ASSESSING

Kogan Page Books for Teacher series
Series Editor: Tom Marjoram

ASSESSING SCHOOLS

__ Tom Marjoram __

Books for Teachers
Series Editor: Tom Marjoram

KOGAN
PAGE

First published in 1989 by Kogan Page Ltd
120 Pentonville Road, London N1 9JN

Typeset by DP Photosetting, Aylesbury, Bucks
Printed and bound in Great Britain by
Biddles Ltd, Guildford

British Library Cataloguing in Publication Data
Marjoram, Tom
    Assessing schools. – (Kogan Page books for teachers)
    1. England. Schools. Assessment
    I. Title
    371.2

    ISBN 1–85091–838–4

Contents

Acknowledgements

I must acknowledge, first of all, the many hardworking and long-suffering teachers, pupils and students whose work I had to inspect and assess over 21 years as an HMI.

I like to think that I got it nearly right on the majority of visits, but I probably learned most from the few who contested my conclusions or even questioned my own assessment methods.

Assessing the work of a school community is a very responsible and complex business. It is an area in which one is more than usually prone to sins of omission and commission, and in which there is always much more to learn; my gratitude, therefore, to shrewder colleagues than myself from whom I also learned so much.

For agreement to quote wiser words and more telling examples than my own I offer thanks to the following:

Alison Hodge for permission to quote from David Hopkinson's book *Edward Penrose Arnold, A Victorian Family Portrait.*

Patrick Taylor of Open Books for permission to quote from *School Matters* by Dr Peter Mortimore and others.

Penguin Books Ltd for permission to quote from *The School That I'd Like* edited by Edward Blishen.

Stuart Maclure, Editor of the *Times Educational Supplement*, for permission to quote the article mentioned on page 18.

Miss A Milford of Oxford University Press for permission to quote from *Lark Rise* by Flora Thompson.

I am also grateful to Mr Eric Bolton, the Senior Chief Inspector, for indicating his assent to my numerous references to HMI reports and publications.

Finally, thanks to Ms Dolores Black and her colleagues at Kogan Page for all their continuing help with this and other books in the series.

Introduction

For some years now our schools have been high on the political agenda. They take the lion's share of local authority rates and a very substantial proportion of central tax revenue as well.

In return, they feed our workforce with new expertise. Without schools there would be no trained personnel to staff our hospitals, factories, offices, service industries and, indeed, schools themselves.

They also influence the behaviour and attitudes of our future citizens for our school-leavers carry with them ideas, attitudes and habits partly acquired at school.

But the equation between what schools cost and what they achieve has always been a complex, some would say an impossible, one. Clearly, there are views, some of them based upon experience, careful study or research, about the optimum size of school; the best class size for this or that age group and activity; the most economic and effective ways of providing accommodation, equipment and resources for this or that subject; the most efficient ways of training teachers for this or that age group, aspect or subject. But given perfect conditions in an 'ideal' school we could never guarantee that all the pupils benefited equally because so many other factors, beyond school control, also affect their learning. Home background, parental expectations, peer group pressures, state of intellectual, emotional and physical growth and health all play a powerful role in school receptivity. So it is virtually impossible to forecast the educational output to be gained from a given input or expenditure.

Consequently, it is easy for the biased, politically motivated mischief-maker or the uninformed outsider to complain that schools cost too much, that teachers get too much pay and holidays, that pupils arrive in work unable to spell properly and/or calculate quickly, or that football hooliganism, street muggings and other social ills arise from the ineffectiveness or negligence of our schools.

Yet with the educational and economic tides of our times running as they do, schools will become more and not less open to criticism and scrutiny.

Since September 1988, the powers of school governing bodies have broadened and increased. The Education Reform Act of 1988 also offers parents the opportunity to opt to take their children's schools out of LEA control and into direct funding by central government and to play a correspondingly increased role in their management, funding and control. Finally, no one believes that the impending poll tax will hit pockets more lightly than existing local rates. All these factors in various ways will intensify the public accountability of schools.

The purposes of this volume is certainly not to teach inspectors how to inspect but to convey some idea of how the trained, experienced and fair-minded professional goes about assessing a school before he/she makes any kind of summative judgement. As will be evident, school assessment is a complicated and time-consuming business but if it succeeds in isolating strengths and weaknesses and some of their causes, it can be a very valuable process. (It is not without significance that, historically, HM inspectors predated the Board of Education.)

Some teachers have been involved in school self-assessment exercises and they may be familiar with the contents of this book. Others who have not may find it helpful in their own 'stock-taking'.

For governors of schools and all others who make judgements about schools it is hoped that this book will offer some useful information and helpful insights which will enable them to discharge their duties wisely and effectively.

Concerned and interested parents who may come upon this book will, hopefully, find that it chimes with their own aspirations and demands of the schools their children attend. Although written largely out of my own teaching and inspecting experience over more than 40 years, I have also attempted to include those aspects which were of peculiar interest to me as a parent.

Finally, I would be delighted if any student or pupil thought it worth reading and writing to me for, in the end, schools are for the learners themselves. These will, of course, include teachers, but the main client body is our rising generation. Many of them already have shrewd and sensible ideas about the world they want to serve and live in. What are their priorities in assessing their schools? I hope I may have succeeded in reflecting some of them in this book.

Chapter 1

Assessing, What, Why and Who?

What is assessment?

I shall take assessment to cover that range of processes by which we collect information in order to 'measure' educational performance of all kinds.

'Measure' in this sense must always be read as in parenthesis, for 'measuring' educational performances and outcomes is very different from weighing out potatoes or selling petrol by the litre.

Two very experienced and well-qualified teachers independently marking the same mathematics examination script are quite liable to differ by a mark or two. Asked to assess the mathematical potential or 'originality' of a mathematics student their judgements would probably diverge even more.

In subjects such as poetry, music or art, which may involve emotional response and where performance criteria are more difficult to define or even agree, the task of assessment can be more complicated still. Indeed, the independent judgements of non-professionals of the same musical performance or the same abstract painting can be totally opposed.

This brings me to my first point: that assessment, to merit the name, must be as *reliable* as possible. That is to say, independent assessments of the same piece of work must agree within tolerable limits. This is usually achieved by prior discussion about exactly what is being assessed, by agreeing a fairly detailed marking scheme and usually by carrying out some pilot marking trials so that over-generous or over-rigorous markers may moderate their standards and bring them more into line with those of other members of the marking panel.

Assessing schools

In this book I shall be concerned primarily with assessing schools. Even the smallest school is a very complex institution. Its overall assessment must to some extent be the sum of a large number of component assessments, for the judgement one accords to such an institution will be formed from assessments of its 'output', ie the work and achievements of its students in many very different areas of the curriculum, its contribution to the community and indeed all those other factors which affect these – its staffing, academic and pastoral organisation, curricular aims, buildings and other resources.

Each of these 'component' assessments is itself a complicated task. Thus, any given student's achievement in, say, English will itself be the sum of individual knowledge and skills acquired in listening, speaking, reading and writing for many purposes and audiences, to say nothing of attitudes to the subject and literary style and tastes acquired. The overall assessment of the school's success in teaching English to all its pupils is a composite of their individual performances.

If we can then bring together the judgements made about all the different subjects taught in a school, its academic and social ethos, its examination and sporting achievements, judged against all the personal and material circumstances in which these are achieved, we may be on the threshold of making a responsible, professional assessment of the whole institution.

The overall assessment is only as reliable and valid as that of the component assessments from which it is adduced.

My second point, therefore, is that assessing schools is a highly professional task and one which can be undertaken too lightly by the uninformed, mischievous and prejudiced with consequential damage.

Evaluation

Terms such as 'judging', 'testing', 'assessing', 'examining', 'inspecting' and 'evaluating' are often used loosely and interchangeably.

In my view, testing and examining are two of the many processes by which educational achievement may be assessed. 'Inspecting', as the word implies, is a process of external assessment which involves a detailed look at all the activities undertaken in the subject or school under inspection.

In his useful book *In-School Evaluation*, Professor Marten Shipman writes:

> The use of a systematic record-keeping and *assessment* system in the school

is an important technique. It is also the main way of accumulating information for *evaluating* the success of the school. (my italics)

'Evaluation' for me, however, is a different matter. In the quotation above I would have used the term 'assessing' instead of 'evaluating' in the last sentence.

In bringing together the many different assessments that may be made of various particular aspects of a school's work, one is still producing an assessment of that school. When that assessment is made known or published, those who read it may react in different ways. Without questioning the assessment itself, one reader might feel that the emphases are misplaced, or that the curriculum offered was deficient (eg computer studies, or home economics or Latin not offered), or that the range of sporting and extra-curricular activities was too restricted, while another might feel that the programme offered was satisfactory and would gladly enrol his or her children at the school.

In setting the assessment against their own personal philosophies, prejudices or likes/dislikes, or even life-styles, people are setting subjective values alongside the more professionally constructed 'objective' assessment to produce their individual *evaluations* of the school described.

Assessment is the process which describes in detail, for example, for how long and how well the Talmud is taught in a school, or how efficiently rifle practice is conducted; it does not concern itself with the *value* of teaching such things at all, whether technology is more valuable than classical Greek, or whether pastoral aims should take priority over academic aims in a school. Such questions lead us into *evaluation* and, while that further process is politically and philosophically interesting and also inevitable, it is not one with which I propose to concern myself in this book.

Thus, the term 'evaluation' will be used sparingly. My stance echoes the terms of reference of the Assessment of Performance Unit (APU) whose task it was to assess and display national performance standards at 11 and 16 in mathematics, language and science – for others to comment upon and *evaluate*.

Why assess?

Of course, assessment cannot always be as detached and uninvolved as my previous statement implies. If, for example, in the course of assessing the work of a school, an inspector, advisor or the head teacher him or herself came across some dangerous practice, or unsafe piece of apparatus, or even some teaching which was factually incorrect, it would be necessary to make immediate comment and take remedial action. Fortunately, such situations occur infrequently. However, it remains the case that although the purposes of assessing students, subjects or schools vary, the process of assessment should nearly always – ours being an imperfect world – result in action of some kind that could effect an improvement. Usually, that action is taken by the assessed, not the assessors.

Different purposes

When assessing the work and progress of an individual child the purpose may be:

1. to see whether sufficient mastery has been acquired to justify moving on to the next concept, or chapter, or class (*criterion referenced assessment*);
2. to pinpoint any particular weaknesses/difficulties and to spot any strengths (*diagnostic assessment*);
3. to compare the child's progress and level of achievement with other children in the same class or national age group (*norm referenced assessment*).

Such purposes are *formative* in that they are designed to inform the next step.

Occasionally, the purpose of a concluding assessment or leaving examination may be primarily intended to sum up a student's achievement to date. Such assessments are *summative* though even here the assessment can often be used to inform the next step – the next school, college or career.

When assessing a whole school, similar motives may be involved. The school itself, or the LEA inspectors or HMI may wish to:

1. check the general efficiency and effectiveness of the school as an educational institution against its own declared aims and objectives;
2. identify its particular strengths and weaknesses;
3. compare it with other schools of its kind locally or nationally.

Here, too, actions ensue. Stock-taking and regular reviews are important to all shops, libraries and businesses and nearly always result in some form of action or changed procedures. Likewise, school reviews or inspections alongside continuous monitoring by the head teacher and staff are crucially important processes and generally result in steady development punctuated by periods of more radical change.

Who assesses schools?

To some degree and for a wide spectrum of reasons, nearly everyone makes a judgement at some time or other about their local comprehensive school, the nearby prep school or indeed the system as a whole. The fact that education and the 1988 Education Reform Act top the political agenda at the time of writing indicates a great interest in, if not concern for, our educational system.

THE PERSON IN THE STREET

The person in the street certainly assesses schools. Pick a citizen at random in a strange town and he or she will tell you immediately which is the 'best school' in the area. If you press further, you may find this opinion is based upon little more than hearsay, local press reports or personal prejudice (he or she went there and/or his or her own youngsters go there!). More tenuously still, it may be based solely on the appearance and behaviour of the pupils on the local streets and buses.

THE PRESS

Reporters find rich copy in our schools. Every newspaper has its educational column and correspondent. Some of the best educational journalists have made significant contributions through their work. Provincial educational press literature often limits itself to Prize Days, exam results and unfortunate incidents. The tabloids seem only interested in strikes, violence and scandals – virtue rates few column inches.

PUPILS

Children undoubtedly assess their own – and other – schools. In the 1967 *Observer* competition which invited secondary school children to describe 'The school that I'd like', and which was the subject of Edward Blishen's book of that title, it emerged that the captive clients of our education system have many cogent comments and constructive things to say.

Gillian, 13, voiced a common concern of her contemporaries when she wrote:

The school I would like would be perfect, glorious in every way, where you wouldn't worry yourself to death over things, wouldn't get bored, and yet wouldn't get lethargic. It would be a friendly school, everyone familiar with everyone, everyone cooperative, with ambitions, big ideas for the future.

Others produced comments and suggestions such as:

Give me a school where discipline, regimentation and good manners are not *everything*.

Our school is like a sausage machine churning out eight-O Level geniuses.

No one would leave until 18 ....

Give us a more varied syllabus ....

Teaching would be imaginative and stimulating ....

In 1969 the *Times Education Supplement* also trawled over 1,000 entries from 7 to 11-year-old pupils on teachers, real or imaginary, loved or loathed. Many of these were about jolly, smiling, helpful and sometimes slightly eccentric teachers but here, too, there were serious and even shrewd comments about such things as different attitudes to boys and girls, the distractions of classroom noise and the lack of opportunity to initiate ideas or discussions:

Whenever a girl gets some work wrong he will say 'Just like girls to get it wrong'.

Then he bangs on the table and drums everything out of your head and shouts at you.

She tells us to be quiet but she never is.

One of the most endearing was in praise of 'Mr King':

If we have a test we don't get nervous about how many we will get because he doesn't really mind as long as we try our hardest. 'Have a go, Joe,' he says.

In my own visits to schools I have frequently come across delightful pieces of writing by children about their own schools.

Seven-year-old Corinne once presented me with a prayer she had written on the back of her spelling test. In lovely, rounded, Marion Richardson script it read:

Our teachers help us
O Lord, please give them the
strength to withstand the noise
Lord, hear us.

Billy Bingham revealed a pleasantly ironic wit in his recollection of the English essay lesson:

TIME
The teacher made us stay quiet
Three minutes.
My life is being wasted.
Three minutes are going by and I am
Just sitting down quietly.
It's boring – the teacher is enjoying it
It's up: the three minutes have passed.
The teacher tells us the title – Time.
Three minutes of my life have been wasted,
And now I am wasting time myself
By writing slowly.
I feel my life has been wasted for no reason
Except waiting and listening to silence;
Golden, mind you–
Not for us, for the teacher.
Billy Bingham (13)

But, of course, and more seriously, pupils have a very significant role to play in school assessment. They alone, after all, are the *clients*, and in no other business are the clients' opinions sometimes so neglected. The present government talks endlessly of *parents'* choice and *parents'* views, but when all is said and done it is not parents who have to sit through incomprehensible lessons or suffer the wrath of scornful taskmasters.

Some schools, and happily a growing number, have Schools Councils upon which class representatives sit and convey their views. Education authorities like the dear, doomed ILEA even instituted pupil-governors.

In my dealings with young people speaking candidly about their schools I have always found them tolerant, understanding, appreciative and often very shrewd in their assessments.

PARENTS
This group certainly assesses schools unendingly and everywhere. And of course they should! Most parents love their children and want the best for them. They know only too well how important qualifications are in our rat race society. Under the 1988 Education Reform Act parents have the right to opt out of LEA control and virtually run schools themselves.

Some welcome this; others view the future with foreboding. For if all

19

is to turn on parental assessment of the school we need to be concerned with how such assessments are made. And, indeed, parents need to be helped to make such judgements in a measured and thorough fashion.

EMPLOYERS

They also assess schools – very often on the slender basis of the particular characteristics of pupils they have employed. I remember a teaching colleague many years ago who was responsible for careers and placement. If a firm new to the area was offering posts he made sure that the first candidate was outstanding. First impressions were vital. Nowadays industry is better informed about schools and the larger firms have long had their own education and training officers and in-house training schemes.

Even so, a common cry from employers is for youngsters who can read, write and do maths. 'We will give them the industrial skills.' However, thanks to Project Technology, and later the Technical and Vocational Education Initiative (TVEI), there is now legislation to include a technological element into the school curriculum for all pupils.

THE PROFESSIONALS

Those people whose job it is to assess schools in some way or another include HM inspectors of schools, LEA inspectors and advisors, and the DES through its Assessment of Performance Unit (APU). The independent school associations have also set up their own accreditation and review system under the aegis of the Independent Schools Joint Council (ISJC). Accreditation and review visits are all led by retired HMI and the process resembles the current inspection procedures of HMI.

How then does the professional assess a school? The detail of this is reserved for Chapter 3 of this book but it needs to be said here that the process is a complex and rigorous one mirroring the great complexity of the institutions assessed.

Every school is different and each must be judged against not only the achievements of its pupils but also against the many other social and material factors and local conditions which may impinge upon its work. Thus, while the main foci in professionally assessing any school in detail are the quality of the pupils' work and the pastoral quality of life of the school as a community, various other factors which affect it must also be taken into account. These include the catchment area, the social mix of the pupils, the affluence and general prosperity of the area, the quality of the buildings and the equipment, the qualification and experience of the staff, the organisation of the school, the links with parents, the community and local industry, and the range of extra-curricular activities and opportunities.

Each of these items, as we shall see, merits a section or even a chapter to itself.

TEACHERS

Perhaps the most interesting group of those who assess, or should assess, schools are the teachers who work in them. Naturally, every good and conscientious teacher since the 1870 Act has worried about his or her work and has sought to improve his or her teaching craft by continuous self-criticism and introspection.

In these days of accountability, rather more overt and formalised procedures are necessary to convince the sceptics. ILEA and Oxfordshire have led LEAs in their systems of school self-assessment. These quinquennial reviews have involved very many secondary schools and have been based on very complex checklists of items which will be discussed later.

In most cases there has been an element of outside moderation or validation but in the end we have had a series of detailed self-assessment reports by the schools themselves. Can the process be valid or even reliable? How can one possibly assess one's own efforts? Some believe the task impossible; others believe that 'responsible' self-critical assessment is the only possible purpose of liberal education. Education is about acquiring independence, self-automation and cutting apron strings. In the end we must all rely upon our own continuing self-monitoring procedures, school assessment likewise.

Essential characteristics of assessment

The salient points about all assessments, including school assessment, may be summarised as follows:

1. Assessments can never be 100 per cent accurate. Assessment in some areas such as aesthetic, and personal and social development, is more difficult than in others.
2. Assessment's most important function is to improve and assist learning and development.
3. Assessment reveals as much about the assessor as about the assessed and should inform and help both.
4. Assessment is an essential part of teaching. It sheds light on what is achieved and what needs to be done next.

5. Assessment is as much concerned with strengths as with weaknesses. It should offer guidance about challenging the able as well as about supporting the less able.
6. Assessment can *ipso facto* generate new ideas.
7. Assessment is not a label but a briefing – it is not a measure of people and children but of their efforts.
8. Assessment requires an ongoing, continuous element.
9. Assessment should make clear what was assessed, the criteria employed, the conclusions reached and their implications for future action.
10. Assessment is worthless if not followed up and acted upon.

The assessment of *whole schools* should, above all, satisfy these principles but we should not forget how complex a task it is. In a sense a school assessment includes all the individual assessments and judgements which are being made daily in every subject, class and sphere of the school's endeavour. But the whole exceeds the sum of the parts and there are larger issues of guiding philosophy or ethos, management and organisation which must also be considered.

In the end, however, assessments can and should only be based upon evidence – the *actual* work of the pupils, those things that the school *claims* to teach – and not the effects of the myriad of influences upon pupils' behaviour from TV, newspapers, parents and other adults and acquaintances outside the school.

Previous national surveys

PRIMARY EDUCATION IN ENGLAND – A SURVEY BY HM INSPECTORS OF SCHOOLS (1978)
This report described aspects of work of 7-, 9- and 11-year-old children in 1,127 classes in 542 schools which were chosen as representative of primary schools in England. It provided information about the schools and the teachers; the classes and their organisation; the curriculum, its planning, continuity and content; the scope and standards of work observed; and it looked at the relationships that appeared to exist between standards of work and locality, type, organisation, teaching methods and staffing.

The conclusions of the report included observations and recommendations about the following:

1. the importance of providing different pupils with work of suitable levels of difficulty;

2. the importance of matching capitation and resources to the size of school;
3. the implications of combining and of leaving separate infant and junior schools;
4. the use of spare classrooms in schools with falling rolls;
5. the importance of offering suitably challenging work in reading and mathematics to able children, who in some schools work at too low a level;
6. the importance of teaching systematically the whole range of reading skills;
7. the task of observational and experimental work in science;
8. the greater contribution that could be made by craft teaching;
9. the lack of progression in history and geography;
10. the very varied range of work offered in primary schools and the fact that narrowing the curriculum to routine work and basic skills proved in most cases a counter-productive policy;
11. the advantages of having music taught by a specialist teacher;
12. the dangers of underestimating the abilities of children from inner city schools;
13. the relative advantages of having one class teacher for all subjects, or sharing the teaching of a class between a number of subject specialist teachers;
14. posts of special responsibility;
15. the role of the teacher as consultant in his or her specialism;
16. the significance of class size;
17. the problems of very small schools;
18. the initial and inservice training of teachers and positive staff development;
19. the importance of assessment and records;
20. the need to raise the expectations which teachers have of children and thus to achieve a clearer definition of the curriculum.

In the decade since these matters were raised there has been some progress towards improving expectations, initial teacher training, inservice training and assessment.

The APU survey reports and particularly those publications which have discussed the implications of the APU surveys in mathematics, language and science, have, with the Cockcroft Mathematics report *Mathematics Counts*, helped teachers to address the Primary Survey criticisms in mathematics, reading and science.

1. *EDUCATION 5–9: AN ILLUSTRATIVE SURVEY OF 80 FIRST SCHOOLS IN ENGLAND (1982)*

2. *9–13 MIDDLE SCHOOLS – AN ILLUSTRATIVE SURVEY* (1983)
3. *EDUCATION 8–12 IN COMBINED AND MIDDLE SCHOOLS, AN HMI SURVEY* (1985)

These three surveys followed close upon the heels of the Primary Survey and looked in particular at those segments of primary education in first and middle schools, and indeed, in surveys 2 and 3, at areas of work by 12- and 13-year-olds previously taught in secondary schools, but since 1966, in some areas, taught in institutions *deemed* primary under the schools regulations.

Rightly, these surveys paid close attention to the peculiar character-istics of first and middle schools of various kinds but they also echoed some of the earlier findings of the Primary Survey.

Thus, in the 5–9 Survey, narrow concentration upon the four rules of arithmetic to the exclusion of their application in problem-solving was noted. It was also remarked that 'able children are rarely given extra help'. The majority of teachers were not primarily trained for the work they were doing and needed extra help. However, by contrast with the Primary Survey there was

> more evidence in the first schools of work intended to help children to understand the physical and natural world and which might develop the children's skills of observation and lead to early scientific understanding.

The 8–12 Survey naturally focused upon such issues as the curriculum of 12-year-olds previously taught in secondary schools, and upon the characteristics of transfer at 8 instead of 7. Many of the schools visited were by their very nature small and so there were questions of curriculum breadth and differentiation, staff levels and teacher deployment.

The 9–13 Middle School Survey provided a detailed study of a representative sample of 48 of these schools out of the 610 existing in January 1983.

The picture revealed many of the same strengths and weaknesses found in inspections of primary and secondary schools and highlighted the problems and advantages of creating two transfer breaks at 9 and 13 where previously there had been one at 11. Poor continuity between phases could affect both 'ends' of the 9–13 school. By contrast, these schools offered the benefits of a gradual, phased transition from primary to secondary schooling. The survey also raised again all the long-standing questions about the age at which children should be introduced to subject teaching and how and when the balance between generalist and specialist teaching should change.

The Primary Survey, the 8–12 and 9–13 Surveys are particularly interesting in that each displays in appendices the methodology employed and lists the detailed items sought and scrutinised in every area of work inspected.

Taken together these surveys provide a detailed account of how large teams of professional inspectors planned, carried out and analysed what they found in the course of assessing large groups of schools and also the individual schools within these groups.

ASPECTS OF SECONDARY EDUCATION IN ENGLAND: A SURVEY BY HM INSPECTORS OF SCHOOLS (1979)

As a companion exercise to the Primary Survey, an almost parallel survey of 384 maintained secondary schools of all types was carried out between 1975 and 1978. This survey concentrated mainly upon the final two years of compulsory schooling. The report deals substantially with language, mathematics, science education and personal and social development, and to a lesser extent with other subjects. Particular attention was paid to 'across the curriculum' issues such as the contribution of all subjects to language development, the application of mathematics to other areas and the links between academic learning and social development.

This survey lists the forms used and type of information gathered. It describes the statistical procedures employed and devotes its fourth appendix to 'gifted pupils'.

The report cannot be summarised and should be read. It offers a whole chapter of general reflections upon major issues arising. Among those were two echoes of the primary and middle school reports:

> There were indications that the ablest pupils were not always sufficiently challenged.
> Particularly, it may be necessary to develop a more explicit rationale of the curriculum as a whole.

A third major point dealt with a concern not shared by earlier surveys, namely the effects of public examinations upon styles of teaching and learning, effects which, at worst,

> produced heavily directed teaching, a preponderance of dictated or copied notes, an emphasis on the giving and recall of information, with little room or time for enquiry or exploration of applications.

Ten years later, the GCSE, with its emphasis on oral work, course work and practical performance, is influencing teaching and learning in different, and it is to be hoped better, ways.

THE APU SURVEYS
The Assessment of Performance Unit was set up at the DES in 1975. Its terms of reference were:

> To promote the development of methods of assessing and monitoring the achievement of children at school, and to seek to identify the incidence of underachievement.

From 1977 it began, with the help of research teams at the National Foundation for Educational Research (NFER), Chelsea College and Leeds University, to conduct national surveys of pupil performance at 11 and 16 in mathematics and language, at 11, 13 and 16 in science, and at 13 in the first foreign language.

The first report on mathematical development at 11 appeared in 1980 and this was followed by many others in all four curriculum areas. In 1985 the DES published a review of all the mathematical survey findings from 1978 to 1982 and, independently, the Cambridge Institute of Education produced *New Perspectives on the Mathematics Curriculum* appraising the same period.

These surveys were concerned neither with assessing *individual* children, nor with assessing individual schools. No single child answered all the test items; different children answered different selections of items. Only a small proportion of the pupils in each of a representative, stratified sample of schools were tested, although numerically the sample (1–2 per cent of the whole age group) was large enough to generate confidence levels of 95 per cent.

Each survey, by aggregating the responses of all the pupils tested, was designed to produce, rather like a completed jigsaw, a meaningful picture of all the separate, meaningless pieces. These final pictures did in fact yield highly illuminating information about a wide range of skills, concepts and processes acquired in all four subjects by children of all abilities throughout England, Wales and Northern Ireland. They pinpointed strengths and weaknesses in the teaching of each subject and pointed towards areas needing targeted inservice training and resources. The surveys, or rather the accompanying item banks of questions and assignments developed, also moved forward the whole methodology of testing in a wide range of areas such as spoken language, oral comprehension, attitude testing, practical mathematics and practical science. Many of the methods of assessment developed could be modified for individual classroom assessment and for school assessment.

Similar international surveys of mathematics have also been

conducted to provide comparisons between standards achieved in various countries.

Thus, the APU and these International Educational Assessments provided a kind of 'national stock-taking' or 'aerial photograph' of important parts of the educational territory. Indirectly, they provided ideas and some techniques for assessing individual schools and individual pupils but they did not, of themselves, produce assessments of individual schools.

Chapter 2

What Aspects of Schools Should be Assessed?

Secondary schools

Most people agree that the main job of secondary schools is to 'educate' their students. However, perceptions of education vary. Many parents and employers expect young people to learn a fairly wide range of skills, concepts and subject matter which will enable them to acquire qualifications and get a job, and which will serve them well and prove useful in life.

Professor BF Skinner in *New Scientist*, 21 May 1964, wrote that 'Education is what survives when what has been learnt has been forgotten.' He therefore seemed to see the task of schools as the transmission of attitudes and values and the inculcation of ways of thinking, analysing and forming one's own opinion.

There is no serious conflict between these two views; they both see schools as being in the business of producing an output which includes academic success, skills and processes learned, intellectual and moral attitudes acquired *together with* social and personal development.

Most of these aims are pursued through the design of the curriculum and its delivery, but other less tangible virtues may be transmitted through the values, customs and general atmosphere of the school and the hidden messages they convey.

It would, therefore, seem that a necessary if not sufficient set of areas which must be looked at individually in order to produce an overall balanced school assessment must include the following:

1. The work of the students in individual subjects of the curriculum.
2. The personal and social education of the students.
3. The staffing of the school: its management and the quality of teaching.
4. The curriculum: its appropriateness, balance, breadth, differentiation and organisation, and its conformity with law.

5. The pastoral care and quality of life in the school.
6. The range and quality of materials, equipment and non-personal teaching resources available.
7. The actual premises within which the school's activities are accommodated and organised.

When HM inspectors publish reports upon individual secondary schools, these seven headings tend to be reversed. A section on the nature and scope of the school is followed by sections on premises, equipment and resources, staffing, academic and social organisation, curriculum, pastoral care, leading up to the heart of the report, namely its assessment of the work of the students and their personal and social development. The report ends with some reference to the school's extra-curricular life and activities, relations with parents, former pupils and the local community, and a conclusion distilling the strengths, weaknesses and principal matters for consideration. This structure is described in greater detail in the next chapter.

Let us look at the seven areas listed above.

1. The work

'I am always for getting a boy ahead in his learning, for that is a sure good.' Most of us would include girls but would accept Dr Johnson's pithy dictum. For central to the school is the work of its pupils.

In a large secondary school each subject department is often examined in detail. Each of these 'subject' assessments merits a book in itself and so only the broadest indications of essential assessment criteria are given at the end of this chapter. What follows is a series of general questions applicable to all or most subjects:

(a) Is/are there a syllabus/syllabuses of work?
(b) Is/are this/these appropriate for the ages and abilities of the students?
(c) Is there an accompanying scheme of work explaining the methodology to be employed and listing textual references?
(d) Is the subject well timetabled and is there sufficient homework set? What form does the latter take?
(e) Is the teaching interesting, lively, clear and sound? Is it accompanied by good presentation – audiovisual material, hand-outs, clear boardwork?
(f) Does classroom discussion offer scope for extended answers, genuine discussion and debate?

(g) Is there an appropriate component of practical, experimental or field work?

(h) Is work well presented? Are notes made by students or copied from the blackboard? Are there opportunities for a wide range of oral and written response – discussion, long responses, short talks; notes, brief reports, speculative accounts, imaginative writing – and so on?

(i) Is work well and regularly corrected? Are difficulties explained and followed up? Are growth points encouraged and developed?

(j) Is there a reasonable quality and range of work covered overall?

(k) Are there any examples of real excellence? Prize-winning performances? How are such efforts used and celebrated?

(l) Is the school work in any subject linked to any extra-curricular or club activity – or to the work in any other subject area – in some unusual or innovative fashion?

(m) Is any of the work open to negotiation with the students?

2. The personal and social development of students

This aspect of a school's output is impossible to measure, and very difficult to assess, without involving moral judgements or even religious views and personal prejudice. For example, is the desired outcome a polite, thoughtful, considerate, deferential, law-abiding student or an articulate, assertive, 'liberated' and unconventional one? Or a bit of both?

Here is the set of questions which I *myself* ask; they are not necessarily the 'right' ones:

(a) Are there opportunities in lessons for students to resolve dilemmas, make moral choices, discuss ethical values for themselves?

(b) Does the school offer opportunities for the exercise of personal responsibility and self-assessment in behaviour and work?

(c) Does the ethos of the school encourage respect for others and a willingness to listen to (and dispute) others' opinions?

(d) Is there a similar 'unspoken respect' for plants, animals and things – particularly other people's property?

(e) Are there opportunities for group work in various situations and also opportunities for the exercise of leadership?

(f) Is there available to every student a counselling, listening, adult ear and a source of private guidance when required for help with careers, work problems, personal relationships and even more serious difficulties?

(g) What is the quality of inter-student, inter-staff and student-staff relationships? Is it strongly hierarchical, overfamiliar ...?

(h) Are there school rules about dress, hygiene, behaviour, movement, transport, conduct outside school?

(i) To what extent are the academic and pastoral organisations of the school linked so as to avoid duplication on the one hand and no man's land gaps on the other?

(j) Who *actually* sets the tone and deliberately fosters – or ensures that *everyone* fosters – this aspect of the school's work?

3. The staffing of the school: its management and the quality of teaching

The questions in the previous section and in this one can hardly be asked by parents or lay persons interested in the school. Most of the information available to inspectors or other professionals must be handled with care and to some extent held in confidence.

In assessing schools most LEA inspectors and all HMI have the right to sit at the back of lessons and scrutinise exercise books. In some schools the headteacher may also visit lessons, and heads of department sometimes watch the lessons of young teachers or students, although in these cases the purpose is not always school assessment. Parents, however, may not sit in on lessons and must judge indirectly. They may see their children's books and whether they are regularly marked, but accounts of lessons and 'what goes on at school' related second-hand by pupils can be unreliable to say the least.

Nevertheless, many school prospectuses list the staff and their qualifications, although this occurs more commonly in the independent school sector. It remains to be seen whether those maintained schools which, in future, choose to opt out of LEA control will begin to advertise their assets more publicly.

In an ideal world, or at least in my world, I would want to know the answers to these questions:

(a) Are all subjects taught by teachers qualified in those subjects? In junior and infant schools, have the teachers been specifically trained for that phase?

(b) In each subject department of the secondary school, is there a senior teacher who is capable of spotting and encouraging outstanding talent? Are there also teachers skilled in helping those who have great difficulty with the subject?

In a primary school, is there a *range* of expertise among the staff such that for every major area of the curriculum – language, mathematics, science, music and the visual arts – there is one teacher who can act as an 'expert' or consultant on the staff?

(c) What is the staffing ratio and how much marking and preparation time is allowed?

(d) How is the teaching load of each department deployed?

(e) Do those who wish to, and are able, take work in the sixth form?

(f) Is there any form of staff appraisal or annual career development review?

(g) Is there induction support for new teachers and inservice training for the more experienced?

(h) How *stable* is the staff as a whole? Is there a good commonroom spirit, or are there cliques and factions?

(i) What are the job descriptions of the deputy heads and senior staff? Are their areas of responsibility clear?

(j) What staff meetings occur and how are these conducted?

(k) What are the relationships in general between pupils and staff? Does their influence extend beyond the classroom?

(l) Are the staff paid on the current national scales and do they enjoy a state pension scheme?

(m) Are all staff indemnified against accident to themselves and/or with students?

Separate questions need to be posed of the headteacher, senior staff and their management:

(n) What is the chain of command? How does the headteacher arrive at and disseminate policy decisions and new procedures?

(o) Are there regular and/or reasonably frequent management meetings between the headteacher and his or her deputies, senior staff, all staff? Are such meetings timetabled and minuted?

(p) Does the headteacher have authority over all/some school finance? Can he or she plan ahead financially?

(q) Can the headteacher appoint new staff and/or promote existing staff? Can he or she terminate appointments?

(r) Are there 'career development' and/or staff appraisal arrangements? What role does the headteacher play? Who appraises him or her?

(s) What is the headteacher's relationship with the governing body?

4. The curriculum

The following are questions that should be asked when evaluating a school's curriculum:

(a) Does it conform to the Education Acts (eg religious education and acts of worship, provision of the three *core* subjects, English, mathematics and science, and the seven other *foundation* subjects, technology, history, geography, art, music, physical education and a modern language?
(b) What other subjects are offered? When?
(c) How is the curriculum of work *timetabled*?
  (i) Is there a suitable *amount* of time allowed for each subject taught?
  (ii) Is the *timing* of sessions appropriate? (or, for example, are all the maths lessons arranged on Thursday and Friday)?
  (iii) Is each subject available in each year of the school, ie progressive from 11–16, or available only at certain stages?
(d) Is the curriculum of work sensibly accommodated in the areas available?
  (i) Science lessons in labs?
  (ii) Dance in the hall or gymnasium?
(e) Are the obvious difficulties such as, eg, games first two periods before dew has risen, swimming immediately after a meal, all mathematics lessons late afternoon, etc avoided?
(f) Is the overall timing and spacing so planned to: suit the reasonable convenience of staff; minimise movement about the school between lessons; avoid the waste of staff time and optimise the use of available space?
(g) Is the timetabling of classes and consequent homework coordinated?

5. Pastoral care

This is closely linked with Section 2. However, in that section we were thinking more of the evident *effect* of the school's provision upon the students – the personal developments and achievements, as it were, that accompanied the academic ones. In this section we interrogate the

33

structures and personnel who are mainly, though not wholly, concerned with pastoral care and personal development.

(a) Are there counsellors, tutors, housemasters and mistresses or such, whose primary role is to exercise pastoral care/guidance/personal supervision?
(b) Are there times (eg form periods, house prayers, etc) and/or places (tutor bases, houses, sanctuaries, careers rooms, etc) associated with the pastoral function?
(c) Is there a careers staff/careers room?
(d) Is there a school doctor/nurse/matron?
(e) Is there a unit or units for the withdrawal of disturbed students or for those with major learning problems?

If a boarding school:

(f) What facilities are available to boarders – dormitories, single, double or treble bedrooms, studies, dayrooms, recreation rooms, hobbies facilities, chapel, sanatorium, clothes and boots stores, wardrobes, cupboards, parking for cycles/cars?
(g) What is the quality of the food and the dietary balance of the menu over the week?
(h) Tuckboxes? Tuckshops? Kitchenette for own cooking?

6. Equipment and resources

'Resources' in general will include teaching and non-teaching staff, but these have been considered under 3. In this section we list only books, materials and apparatus.

BOOKS
The following points need to be raised concerning this resource:

(a) Are there a sufficient number and wide enough range of text, reading and reference books in all subjects?
(b) How are these stored/housed – book storerooms, class libraries, subject department libraries, central library or book area?
(c) Does 'library' stock include maps, plans, videotapes, sound tapes or similar reference material? How is it catalogued?
(d) Is there a librarian and/or library assistants? Do students assist with books/library duties?

MATERIALS
Does the school keep sufficient exercise books, graph books, writing

and drawing paper, paint, clay, wood/timber/metal, chemicals, fabrics, food?

APPARATUS

The lack of significant items of apparatus such as a kiln in pottery, electronic balance in chemistry, pedestal drill in the workshops, trampoline in PE, etc will show up in subject assessments.

The purpose of this section is to collate separate subject comments about apparatus to produce an overall picture of the school's stock of equipment.

7. Premises

Usually the first and most obvious asset of a school is its building(s) and site. No wonder that some of our more famous schools are remarkably imposing edifices.

School prospectuses often list the staff and their qualifications and describe the curriculum and sporting facilities offered. The main impact of such documents, however, is usually the gallery of photographs of the school's facade and choicer specialist laboratories, workshops and drama/art studios, but they seldom show the shabbier side and never reveal whether there are *enough* laboratories to permit *all* or most science lessons to be timetabled in them. This point will apply with particular force when the considerably increased legal requirements for science and technology come into force.

The professional assessor will, therefore, look for the usual range of classrooms, laboratories, photographic dark rooms, workshops, computer rooms, gymnasium and changing rooms, commerce room and home economics areas. He or she will also look for soccer, rugby, hockey and netball pitches, for covered sports facilities, running track, jump pitches, nets, tennis and squash courts. There may even be golf and riding facilities and all-weather playing surfaces.

But he or she will also ask about:

(a) the arithmetical sufficiency of laboratory and other space. (Eg given a five-form entry, 11–16 school in which every student is timetabled for eight periods a week of science, the fifth form alone will require 5×8 laboratory periods. This will exhaust the total availability of one laboratory in a 40-period week. *Five* laboratories would theoretically suffice although in practice six would be necessary for a five-form entry school. Similar

35

calculations are necessary in respect of PE (in the gym), art (in the art studio), etc);

(b) the design and safety of working spaces, eg
locks on kilns
guards on lathes
plugs near water supplies
slippery floors around drills and saws
fume cupboards
fire escapes, extinguishers and blankets;

(c) the general state of decoration and repair of the premises, the roof, drains, pathways and playing surfaces.

BOARDING ACCOMMODATION

Such accommodation of the kind found in many independent and some state schools presents a further set of questions:

(d) Are dormitories overcrowded (easily achieved where a policy of double-bunking has been implemented)? Spacing of beds, lockers, cupboards? Recreation facilities?

(e) Lighting/heating adequate?

(f) Fire escape?

(g) Proximity and adequacy of bathing and toilet facilities?

(h) Provision for sanatorium and possible isolation?

(i) Laundry?

(j) Matron's room and dispensary – security of medicines, etc?

(k) Provision of kitchens, food stores, food preparation areas and sinks?

Occasionally, unusual items of accommodation and equipment are seen. I personally recall the following unusual items:archery butts, a carillon loft, a bell ringers' loft, pistol and rifle shooting ranges, fives courts, robotics laboratories, electroplating bath, wind tunnel laboratory and planetarium. While, of course, in specialist schools one finds: ballet studios, music practice rooms and even electronic music laboratories. One must, of course, be prepared to scrutinise the organisation, maintenance and safety of all such facilities, however unusual.

The range of provision in a school can be very wide, varying from the lavish with no expense spared to the danger level at which the lack of essential staff, resources and premises begins to jeopardise the quality of education by actually denying opportunity or practical experience in core subject areas.

The annual HMI expenditure reports which for many years have surveyed the state of provision in the maintained sector have played a vital safeguarding role in state schools. As recently as 1987, some serious deficiencies were noted in the fabric of our nation's schools, and also in supplies of books and equipment.

The 'watch dog' role in independent schools has, in recent years, been developed by the ISJC Accreditation, Review and Consultancy Service.

High standards are maintained and more than one school has failed to gain accreditation purely upon the lack of science accommodation or reference books.

A recent HMI survey of secondary schools

In 1988, HMSO published *Secondary Schools, An Appraisal by HMI*. It is worth recalling, however, that this survey, based on a random sample of 185 schools inspected between 1982 and 1986 and intended to provide a mid-1980s snapshot of the nation's secondary schools just before the 1988 Education Reform Act, used the kind of criteria discussed above and carried as its main conclusion that about a quarter of the nation's secondary schools are performing less than 'satisfactorily' and/or give cause for concern. It hastened to add that the evidence did not, however, support a view of secondary education in crisis or rapid decline:

- The standards of work generally were said to be rising 'slowly but erratically' since the secondary survey of 1979. Three-quarters of the 8,000 teachers seen were thought to have unreasonably low expectations of pupils.
- Pedagogical styles generally were not thought to have altered significantly since 1979.
- Standards of numeracy were generally satisfactory but writing was limited in range and oral work disappointing. Curricula in many schools did not provide a 'coherent or systematic aesthetic experience'.
- Not unexpectedly, in the first year of GCSE teachers were reported as being unduly concerned with exams and pupils 'overprepared' by overteaching and excessive notetaking.
- Libraries were pinpointed as the weakest aspect of schools' resources, and textbook provision generally was unsatisfactory in over one-third of all schools.
- Half the schools were poorly decorated and one-third poorly maintained.

- On a brighter note the inspectors found disorder in classrooms rare. 'The behaviour of pupils was often extremely good and they were generally cooperative.'

Work in individual subjects

It is a complex enough matter to look at general aspects of the work of a school as we did on pages 29–36. Yet in each different subject area there is a whole list of specific criteria of quality peculiar to that subject.

Thus, if books had not been written already, a book could be written solely on the assessment of, say, mathematics teaching, or on art education. It is not my intention to include in this book what is readily available elsewhere, but I offer below a personal view of some of the points that need to be borne in mind when looking at the main curriculum areas.

ENGLISH
The following points should be considered when assessing English teaching in schools:

1. Opportunities inside and outside the classroom for listening and for oral expression.
2. Extent and variety of reading of individual pupils.
3. Attention to specific reading skills of decoding, comprehension, inference, comparison, skim reading and reading in depth.
4. Provision of texts and library books and relation of reading programmes to pupils' other curricular interests and activities.
5. Reading records.
6. Poetry – read and/or learned? Written?
7. Drama – range of work covered, practical free drama, theatrical work.
8. Writing – experience of continuous writing for various audiences; transactional and expressive writing – narrative, explanation, description, argument and other purposes.

   For younger children, the teaching of handwriting, current conventions of spelling and punctuation, paragraphing, précis, paraphrase and presentation.
9. Relation of language to media of the press, magazines, TV, video.
10. Current technology – tape-recording, telephone usage, wordprocessing, fax machines, etc.

MODERN LANGUAGES

These general points will help to give an overview of a school's modern language teaching methods:

1. Aural work, listening and speaking, pronunciation, interaction – are these an integral part of every lesson?
2. Reading – is there regular use of suitable texts for comprehension, vocabulary, idiom and grammar and to extend the pupil's knowledge of the country concerned?
3. Written work – exercises, free composition, letter and essay writing (for older pupils).
4. Contact with native speakers – assistants, visitors to school, audiovisual material, foreign visits and exchanges.
5. Linguistic activities such as choral repetition, question and answer, mini-dramas and role-play, group scenes.

MATHEMATICS

The content of the school mathematics curriculum was the subject of the Cockcroft Report, *Mathematics Counts*, published by HMSO in 1982.

The report recommended a core content but stressed in paragraph 243 the importance of opportunities for:

- exposition by the teacher;
- discussion between teacher and pupils and between pupils themselves;
- appropriate practical work;
- consolidation and practice of fundamental skills and routines;
- problem-solving, including the application of mathematics to everyday situations;
- investigational work.

More recently, following the royal assent of the 1988 Education Report Act, which calls for assessment at 7, 11, 14 and 16, the DES Mathematics Curriculum Group, working within the framework put forward by the Task Group on Assessment and Testing, has produced the ten-level programme reproduced below.

LEVEL	NUMBER	ALGEBRA	MEASURES	SHAPE AND SPACE	DATA HANDLING
1	Numbers to at least 10. Conservation of numbers. Addition and subtraction with numbers no greater than 10. Estimation of numbers.	Repeating patterns.	Comparison of various quantities: length, weight, capacity ...	2-D and 3-D shapes. Position described in everyday language. Movement along a line.	Sorting objects. Recording directly with real objects or drawings. Simple mapping diagram.
2	Numbers to at least 100. Everyday fractions such as a half and a quarter. Addition and subtraction facts up to 10. Multiplication and division involving numbers up to 30. Estimation of a number of objects up to 30.	Patterns in addition and subtraction facts up to 10. Odd and even numbers. Box notation for an unknown numbers.	Non-standard measures in length, capacity, weight and time. Most commonly used units for these quantities	Everyday shapes such as squares, rectangles, circles, triangles, cubes, rectangular boxes and spheres. Types of movement: straight (translation), turning (rotation) and flip (reflection)	Classification of objects. Simple data collection sheet. Frequency tables. Block graphs. Diagrams to represent classification based on two different criteria. Outcomes of events which are certain/uncertain.
3	Numbers to at least 1000. Decimal notation as a conventional way of recording in money. Negative whole numbers. Addition and subtraction facts to 20. Multiplication facts up to 5 × 5 and in 2, 5 and 10 multiplication tables. Approximation to the nearest 10 or 100. Remainders in the context of calculation.	Number patterns and equivalent forms of 2-digit numbers. Divisibility tests for 2, 5 and 10. Simple function machines.	Wider range of metric units. Appropriate units and instruments. Estimation based on metric units.	Basic properties of 2-D and 3-D shapes. Reflective symmetry in 2-D and 3-D. Compass bearings (8 points).	Information from tables and lists. Bar charts. Graphs where the symbol used represents a group of units. Simple computer database. Likelihood of events: 'events', 'fair' and 'unfair'
4	Whole numbers of any size. Decimal notation to two decimal places in the context of measurement. Simple fractions and percentages. Multiplication tables or facts up to 10 × 10. Multiplication of any whole number by multiples of 10. Addition and subtraction of 2- and 3-digit numbers. Multiplication and division of 2-digit number by a single-digit number. Estimation and approximation to check the validity of calculations.	Doubling and halving applied to fractions including the equivalence of fractions. Simple formulae, functions, equations and inequalities expressed in words. Multiplication and division as inverse operations. Coordinate representation of points in the first quadrant.	Relationships between units. Scale in maps and drawings. Area and volume.	Construction of simple 2-D and 3-D shapes. Measurement of angle. Location on maps specified by means of coordinates (including grid references). Rotational symmetry.	Grouped discrete data, frequency tables and block graphs. Mean and range of a set of data. Line graphs. Interpretation of pie charts. Probability scale from 0 to 1 or 0 to 100%.

LEVEL	NUMBER	ALGEBRA	MEASURES	SHAPE AND SPACE	DATA HANDLING
5	Relationships between place values in whole numbers. Index notation to express parts of whole numbers. Unitary ratios such as 1:50. A range of fractions and percentages. Multiplication and division of single-digit multiples of powers of 10 with whole number answers. Calculations with negative numbers. Trial and improvement methods. Approximation using significant figures or decimal places.	Primes, multiples, factors, squares, square roots and cubes. Sequences of numbers. Formulae, functions, equations and inequalities in symbolic form. Coordinates in all four quadrants.	Common Imperial units still in use and their approximate metric equivalents	Congruence of simple shapes. Properties associated with intersecting and parallel lines and triangles. Networks, symmetries of various shapes.	Grouped continuous data, frequency tables and block graphs. Observation sheets. Computer database. Construction of pie charts. Conversion graphs. Flow diagrams without loops. Randomness. Probabilities based on statistical evidence and probabilities based on assumptions.
6	Relationships between place values in numbers including decimals. Equivalence of fractions and ratios. Conversion of fractions to decimals and percentages. Fractional and percentage changes. Estimation and approximation for checking multiplication and division of whole numbers.	Rules for generating sequences in number. The role of counter-example in disproving a rule. The difference method for exploring the pattern of a sequence. Trial and improvement methods for the solution of linear and simple polynomial equations. Simple inequalities in a number line. Cartesian coordinates to represent simple function mappings.	Compound measures such as speed and density. Formulae for perimeter, area and volume of common shapes. Conversion from one metric unit to another.	Angle and symmetry properties of triangles, quadrilaterals and polynomials. Two-dimensional representation of 3-D objects. Traversibility of networks. Enlargement by a whole number scale factor.	Opinion and fact finding surveys using questions requiring yes/no responses. Scatter graphs for both discrete and continuous variables; correlation. Two-way tables. Network diagrams. Identification of outcomes of combined events which are independent. The sum of the probabilities of mutually exclusive events is 1 or 100%.
7	Numbers in standard index form using positive and negative integer powers of 10. Reciprocals of numbers. Multiplication and division by single-digit multiples of any power of 10. Memory and bracket facilities of a calculator.	Symbolic notation to express the rules of sequences. Complex number patterns. Rules of indices for possible integer values. Wide range of formulae, functions and linear inequalities. Solution of simultaneous linear equations using graphical and other methods.	Recognition of degrees of error in measurement.	Pythagoras' Theorem. Classification and definition of types of quadrilaterals. Mathematical similarity. Vector notation. Enlargement by a fractional scale factor.	Specification and testing of a simple hypothesis. Frequency distributions and frequency polygons. Mean, median, range and interquartile range. Flow diagrams with loops. Relative frequency as an estimate of probability.

LEVEL	NUMBER	ALGEBRA	MEASURES	SHAPE AND SPACE	DATA HANDLING
8	Index notation to represent powers and roots. Calculation with numbers expressed in standard form. Negative numbers in formulae. Calculation involving fractions. Estimation and approximation for checking any type of calculation.	Relationships between powers and roots. Manipulation of simple algebraic expressions. Rules of indices for fractional and negative values. Recognition of the form of graphs of linear, quadratic and reciprocal functions. Straight line graphs to locate regions given by linear inequalities.	Length, area and volume in calculations of plane and solid shapes.	Sine, cosine, tangent and Pythagoras' Theorem in 2-D contexts. Locus of an object moving subject to a rule. Position in 3-D coordinates.	Opinion and fact finding surveys which elicit 3 or more responses to the questions. Cumulative frequency table and cumulative frequency curve. Histograms. Calculation of the probability of a combined event involving two independent events using tabulation or tree diagrams.
9	Positive integers expressed as products of prime numbers. Rational and irrational numbers. Calculation of upper and lower bounds in the addition, subtraction, multiplication and division of two numbers expressed to a given degree of accuracy.	Growth and decay rates. General laws expressed in symbolic form. Interpretation of straight line law ($y = mx + c$). Solution of quadratic equations using graphical methods.	Lengths of arcs, areas of sectors and segments of circles. Surface areas of cylinders, and volumes of cones and spheres.	Trigonometric ratios used in 3-D work. Surface areas of similar figures and volumes of similar figures. Laws of addition and subtraction of vectors.	Presentation of complex data in a simplified form using a variety of diagrams and graphs. Tree diagrams to illustrate the combined probability of several events.
10	Calculation of the upper and lower bounds in addition, subtraction, multiplication and division involving more than two numbers to a given degree of accuracy.	Analysis of the convergence of a sequence, given iteratively, using a calculator or computer. Algebraic manipulation as needed in a variety of contexts. Gradients to a curve and area under the curve using approximate methods. Graphs of functions derived from other functions.	Error analysis of calculations involving measurements.	Angle properties of circles. Graphs of sine and cosine functions for all angles. Combinations and inverses of transformations.	Critical path diagrams.

SCIENCE

The DES Science Working Group, building upon the earlier work of the APU working group, has also in August 1988 developed its own criteria.

The programmes of science study recommended for the National Curriculum 5-16 are divided into four stages for ages 5-7, 7-11, 11-14 and 14-16. Developed progressively throughout these four stages are the skills of exploration, investigation and communication. The contexts in which these develop are described in detail in the Science Working Group's report. In brief, 5- to 7-year-olds learn to observe, collect, handle and find out at first hand about animal and plant life; themselves; waste products; inanimate materials and the effects upon them of heating, cooling, pouring, bending; magnetic materials; batteries and bulbs; food; temperature; sounds; light and weather.

The 7- to 11-year-olds begin to learn the conventions involved in using diagrams, tables, charts, graphs, symbols, etc, and the use of books. At this stage there will be more careful studies of and experiments with phenomena of various kinds, simple surveys and experiments. The children's work with plants and animals, themselves, inanimate materials, heat, light and sound, force and energy, will become more careful, controlled and varied.

Between 11 and 14, there should be opportunities for planning and execution of a variety of investigations and tasks extending considerably the skills and techniques used earlier. More complex topics and processes such as cell formation, food assimilation and use, respiration, reproduction, photosynthesis, bacteria, enzymes, viruses, chemical changes, classification of the elements, geology, water and its phases, electricity, magnetism, energy sources and control, hearing, vision and simple optics and the solar system will be dealt with.

From 14-16, work will be based upon the GCSE syllabuses available.

Assessment will concern itself with how this work is covered but perhaps even more so with the mode of its delivery and organisation and the attitudes produced.

OTHER SUBJECT AREAS

The assessment of all other subjects or areas of the curriculum could be described in equal detail. The content and skills peculiar to each area clearly vary and detailed checklists need to be compiled, or indeed are already available, in books concerned with the teaching of these subjects. However, it is the unique contribution which each makes to general learning that needs to be evident to the assessor and, indeed, the pupils.

Thus, *art* must offer ways of recording experiences and thoughts in visual form and opportunities to express oneself and appreciate the expressions of others through drawing, painting, modelling, collage, print-making, fabric work, etc. *Music* must afford generous opportunity to listen to, record, perform and create impressions and feelings in the form of sound artifacts.

History is about understanding time sequence and chronology, change and continuity, causality and the various types of evidence we use to learn about people in the past.

It used to be said that history is about chaps and geography about maps and indeed my own childhood memories strongly associate roll maps and globes with this subject. However, *geography* is now far broader in compass and should be seen to offer a study of the location, distribution and movements of people – their environment, customs and activities and the ways in which they adapt to, are changed by, or change their environment.

The assessment of *religious education* can present difficulties. Where its purpose is to convey knowledge and interest in the historical development of the church, the meaning of faith for Christians and followers of other religions and various forms of worship, it is no more contentious than history. However, in a denominational school whose aim is to inculcate faith and develop commitment, the assessor may find it more difficult to be objective and detached. For example, a Christian's or a Moslem's assessment of the religious teaching in an orthodox Jewish school might be received with interest but would hardly be accepted seriously. For this reason, on HMI full inspections of denominational schools, religious education was not inspected unless requested. Interestingly enough, I recall several Catholic schools who asked for their religious education to be inspected. In one case the RE inspector was a Lutheran but nevertheless his comments were warmly received and deemed to have been very helpful.

The art of this and indeed all professional assessment must be a judicious mixture of interest, empathy, objectivity and detachment. To a lesser degree this conflict between head and heart can arise in judging works of art or music. Personal taste and inner beliefs and feelings are one thing and cannot be ignored, but they should play very little part in assessing schools.

INTEGRATED CURRICULA
Sometimes, but not often, a secondary school's curriculum is conceived

not in subject terms and divisions, but in curriculum areas such as 'humanities', 'design', 'integrated science', 'business studies', 'communications' or 'environmental studies'. Where a school has planned and programmed its work in such terms it should be assessed on that basis.

If, for example, the environmental studies syllabus in a school contains elements of science, history and geography then, of course, the historical aspects must be taught as well as if they were being taught under the label of history. Likewise the science and geography components must be equally sound. Of equal importance, however, is whether those separate components actually cohere and mutually reinforce and, together, produce an educational whole that offers more than the sum of the parts. This will involve a range of further issues and questions.

The idea of reassembling the contents of the traditional subject curriculum into modules, courses or packages of associated knowledge and skills is sound. Industrial applications and new areas of research are more likely than formerly to involve two or more subject areas. Indeed, many occur at the boundaries of subjects – to such a degree that new 'subjects' like econometrics or mathematical biology are born from time to time.

Chapter 3

Assessing the School as a Whole

What makes a good school?

In Chapter 2 I discussed some of the separate aspects of a school which might in various ways influence its effective and efficient operation. Such factors probably need to be looked at before making an overall judgement about the institution as a whole.

Inspectors and other professionals often have access to such detail but pupils, parents and other people interested in their local schools may have to form their views on more slender evidence. Moreover, they may have widely differing ideas about the *essence* of a good school.

Here are a few anonymous remarks and quotations collected at random. Another set would have been quite different and little can be concluded from such a selection. They do, however, illustrate the widely varying opinions that people express when asked 'What makes a good school?'

A cooperative environment in which the talents of each child can be developed to the full. – *a parent*

Purpose, planning, evaluation and an ear for the parents. – *a teacher*

One that imparts not so much skills as understanding on the basis of which skills can be acquired when needed. – *an employer*

Reading, writing and manners. – *a senior citizen*

One that trains you for life. – *a senior pupil*

One where the teachers don't shout at us. – *a junior pupil*

'The fire 'i the flint shows not till it be struck'. One of the purposes of education is to strike the fire from the flint. Every boy and girl has something in them to be brought out, something they can do really well. But too many flints have not been struck. That's the really dreadful waste. – *Mr Kenneth Baker, Secretary of State for Education and Science*

As it happened, no one in this set of replies stressed good GCSE results, but implicit in most views was the feeling that academic success, if not sufficient in itself, is nevertheless a necessary condition.

How did HM inspectors assess schools?

HM inspectors of schools are still appointed by the Queen in Council and they predate the Ministry of Education itself.

The earliest inspectors, funded by the House of Commons, were appointed in 1839. They were Dr Kay Shuttleworth, Rev Mr Allen and Mr Tremenheare. Though few in number, they made considerable impact, drawing attention to deficiencies in schooling and raising questions which paved the way towards public education.

By 1861, the number of HMIs had grown but they were made subject to the provisions of the 'Revised Code' and responsible for the payment of grants to schools based on the individual examination by an HMI, or his assistant inspector, of individual children. Folk memories of 'the Code' were so ingrained that years after it was abandoned I found myself as a young HMI, when visiting small rural schools, being expected to test all the children, approve the timetable and sign the logbook!

The Act of 1870 enormously enlarged the scope of public education and decreed that all schools should be open to regular inspection by HMI. Until 1895 it became practice for every school to undergo an annual inspection on a prescribed day. By then, the number of subjects taught had increased and to a large number of elementary schools had been added some teacher training colleges, night schools and higher grade schools. The 1902 Act created a framework within which much of modern education in England developed. In 1871 there were 82 HMIs and by 1902 there were 409 central government inspectors of education of various kinds – though not all HMIs.

In 1922 the size of the Inspectorate was 383 and the senior grade of Staff Inspector with national responsibility for certain subjects and aspects of education had been introduced. In the later 1920s the Inspectorate was organised into territorial divisions under Divisional Inspectors and the post of Senior Chief Inspector was instituted.

The Welsh Inspectorate grew from the same beginnings as the English but in 1907 was placed under the Welsh Office and the Welsh

Inspectorate was co-ordinated under its own Chief Inspector working closely with English colleagues. The Scottish Inspectorate is even more distanced and operates autonomously under its own Senior Chief Inspector. In England, in spite of the development of a hierarchy, the grade of assistant Inspector lingered on until 1944 when it was finally abolished.

From the end of the war, as a result of the great increase of educational provision brought about by the 1944 Act, the Inspectorate began to grow and its numbers reached 527 by 1949. One of the clauses of the 1944 Act required Ministers (later Secretaries of State) to 'cause inspections to be made of every educational establishment', including all maintained and independent schools, colleges of education, establishments of further education and the Youth Service (but not universities). This primary duty of reporting to the Secretary of State on the state of education continued to the present day.

Instructive and amusing accounts of those early years of the service are to be found in the writings of Sneyd-Kinnersley and Swinburne. Nineteenth-century HMIs certainly seem to have been a varied bunch. In Flora Thompson's *Lark Rise* we read:

> Her Majesty's Inspector was an elderly clergyman, a little man with an immense paunch and tiny grey eyes like gimlets. He had the reputation of being 'strict' but that was a mild way of describing his autocratic demeanour and scathing judgement ... He looked at the children as if he hated them and at the mistress as if he despised her!

By contrast, the great Matthew Arnold's brother, also an HMI, has been beautifully biographed in David Hopkinson's *Edward Penrose Arnold, A Victorian Family Portrait*:

> Edward Arnold's inspection visits ... presented an image of genial humanity. His feelings for nature, his interest in the state of society, his sympathy for the weak, his humour, 'a fine cheerfulness of life and nobleness of manner', were noted.

How do HM inspectors assess schools nowadays?

The reader who seeks a detailed account of HM inspectors' *modi operandi* will find much in HMI's own official publications. Available from the DES Publications Despatch Centre at Stanmore, Middlesex, are *Reporting Inspections, the Sequels to HM Inspectors Today: Standards in Education* and the Secretary of State's policy statement, *The Work of HM Inspectorate in England and Wales*, which were published after the Rayner study in 1983. These documents make clear that HMI's role is threefold. The Inspectorate (1) assesses standards and trends and advises the Secretary of State on the performance of the system nationally; (2) identifies and makes known good practice and promising developments while drawing attention to weaknesses; and (3) provides advice and assistance to those with responsibilities for institutions in the system through day-to-day contacts, contributions to training, and its own publications. It is not HMI's task to right what is wrong: it is for others to act upon its assessments.

In my own 21 years' service in the Inspectorate I took part in many short, one-day visits, full inspections of primary and secondary schools, specialist subject surveys, the national primary, middle and secondary surveys, visits to teacher-training institutions of all kinds, and was involved in four 'whole LEA' inspections. I also helped to inspect several schools overseas.

Each exercise was different. Each was carefully planned and tailor-made. Many were based upon a carefully devised *aide-mémoire* or schedule of items of the kind shown in Annex B of *Primary Education in England – A Survey by HM Inspectors of Schools* (HMSO, 1978) and in Appendix 4 of *9–13 Middle Schools – An illustrative survey* (HMSO, 1983). But irrespective of the particular exercise there were certain common factors. Above all, we looked at the *quality of the students' work*; we did not make personal comments about teachers.

In watching hours of teaching and in combing through piles of exercise books or pupils' folders of work we looked for characteristic strengths, weaknesses and trends, and were constantly seeking to relate these to staffing, buildings, resources and provision, academic and pastoral organisation, school climate and leadership. Eventually, from a welter of observations would emerge a handful of issues – strengths and weaknesses – upon which the life and work of the school or institution seemed to turn. Many discussions could then follow and a careful, balanced report emerge. From 1984 these reports were nearly all published.

Assessment procedures vary with institutions. A primary school is a very different institution from a secondary one. The two call for different approaches, different teams, different *aide-mémoires* and different reports.

Primary schools

One enjoyable and instructive way of learning what HMIs look for in primary schools would be to read *Primary Schools – Some Aspects of Good Practice* which appeared in 1987.

Key elements of learning, say the inspectors, include knowledge, skills, concepts and attitudes in science, history and geography, mathematics, English and drama. In each of these areas pupils are expected to enlarge their factual knowledge, develop the linguistic, numerical and manipulative skills to control and direct their own learning, acquire concepts which help them to generalise, organise, relate ideas and make judgements, and develop attitudes of enquiry and attention and habits of observation and cooperation which foster learning. Thus, in the primary school HMIs would look first for evidence of these things in the work and learning of the children. Where knowledge is thin or skills insecure or progress too slow or attitudes unfavourable, further matters need to be examined – the books, materials and equipment available, the schemes of work, the organisation of the work in each class and of the classes within the school, the experience and competence of the teachers and the way they work together, the actual premises and, of course, the overall management and quality of leadership and relationships that exist between headteacher, teachers, pupils and parents.

These procedures are not new. In the HM inspectors' handbook I was given in 1966 one of the passages I underlined and never forgot was the following:

The kind of questions most frequently in an inspector's mind, but not necessarily asked, during a visit will be:

'What are the aims of the school, are these of a sufficiently high quality, and how far is it achieving these aims?'

'What and how much are the children finding out for themselves: what are they learning from this and is it worth the while?'

'What first-hand experiences has it been possible to give the children?'

'What opportunities are they given to make use of what they learn?'

'Are the children encouraged to use books of good quality?'

'Are the children making the progress that might be expected of them?'

'Is there continuity in the work within one class and from one class to another and from one stage to another?'

'Does the school care for all sides of the children's development not forgetting the imaginative?'

An LEA survey of junior education

In 1988 the findings of an ILEA survey of 2,000 pupils in 50 primary schools was published as *School Matters – The Junior Years* (Open Books) by the researchers Dr Peter Mortimore and others. Its main emphasis was on junior education.

The range of quality revealed was remarkable, the gap between excellent and poor unacceptably wide. The variation in teaching time alone meant that some pupils received half a day's more teaching each *week* than some others.

Overall, it appeared that the best schools displayed many of the following characteristics. The acceptably good displayed at least nine of them:

1. A voluntary school with no more than 160 children in classes no larger than 24.
2. An experienced headteacher with a good deputy.
3. Low staff turnover.
4. Well-decorated classrooms and adequate play areas.
5. Wide catchment areas.
6. 'Junior' school integrated with and not separated from its infant school.
7. Seven-year-olds arriving able to read.
8. Teachers keeping individual pupil records and forward lesson plans.
9. Staff involved in policy-making.
10. Judicious balance between class teaching and individual instruction.
11. Tactful and generally non-interventionist style by head teacher.
12. Well-focused inset for staff.
13. Broad curriculum avoiding narrow '3 Rs' approach.
14. More praise than punishment.
15. Genuine parental involvement – beyond normal PTA activity.

Secondary schools

The secondary school is larger and more complex than the primary school though its aims, of which more later, differ little in broad developmental terms.

HM inspectors' reports on secondary schools, examples of which are freely available from the DES Publications Despatch Centre at Honeypot Lane, Stanmore, Middlesex, follow a broadly common pattern. The scene is usually set by a section on the *nature and scope* of the school, its location, catchment, size, nature, status (whether independent, voluntary, country), and whether single sex or mixed.

This section also comments upon the admission procedures, the schools from which pupils come, the educational institutions or the forms of employment to which they go afterwards.

The governing body and its activities may be briefly noted together with some reference to finance, and for independent schools, fees and other charges.

The next section will be concerned with the school buildings and playing fields, their state of maintenance and their adequacy to the task of the school.

This is sometimes followed by an evaluation of the equipment and resources available in laboratories, art and craft rooms, gymnasium and home economics areas, and of the supply of stationery, materials and books throughout the school.

No HMI report ever includes personal remarks about members of the teaching or ancillary staff, but there is always an assessment of the match and adequacy of the teaching team, the inservice and induction training available, and their organisation and lines of command and communication.

In an independent school report mention will be made of pension and insurance arrangements, and in a boarding school of the organisation of boarding, catering, housekeeping and health care available.

This section is usually followed by a description and assessment of the organisation of the school, the class sizes, whether streamed, setted or arranged by mixed ability or age. School assemblies, tutor periods, extra-curricular activities, homework arrangements and general disciplinary procedures are also sometimes dealt with at this point.

The next two sections focus upon the *raison d'être* of the whole inspection exercise. The first is usually a major account of the curriculum offered and of the standards of work and the school's other academic, cultural and sporting achievements. The second deals with the personal and social development of the pupils relating this closely to the pastoral care exercised and quality of life apparent in the school.

These sections are followed by detailed assessments of the work in each subject taught, and the report rounds off with some references to out of school activities, school trips, camps and plays, links with parents and old pupils and the community generally. The final paragraph is a conclusion within which are distilled the strengths, weaknesses and the principal issues arising at the time of the inspection.

Ten good schools

One enquiry which addressed the question 'What makes a good school?' in such a way as to inform the public how HM inspectors assess schools was the HMI series: Matters for Discussion No 1, *Ten Good Schools – A Secondary School Enquiry.* (DES, 1977) Visiting panels of inspectors gave attention to seven aspects of schools: their fundamental objectives and the extent to which these were attained in behaviour and academic achievement; pastoral care and its organisation in the school; curriculum and the organisation thereof; staffing and quality of work; the use of premises and resources; links with parents, employers and other members of the local community; and the quality of leadership and resultant ethos in the school.

The ten schools which impressed HMI on these seven counts all strove, in most cases successfully, for good relationships and tension-free discipline; the development of self-confidence and self-respect; the acquisition of knowledge and skills in terms of literacy, numeracy, aesthetic sensibility and physical well-being; the perception through the curriculum of social, moral and religious values and standards for healthy living – and all these things in a context which took account of what had gone before at the primary stage and, through careers education, what was to come in the world of work or continued education.

In many cases these ideals were achieved to a considerable extent by deliberate planning, detailed knowledge of the pupils, and by the organisation of effective structures of cooperation and discipline, and clear channels of communication.

Thus, these good schools gave careful thought to their systems of record-keeping and pastoral care. They all accepted examination requirements as legitimate goals, but took care to ensure that these did not dominate the programme, distort the balance of the curriculum or set unrealistic targets for pupils.

Each school valued its staff and consciously fostered the quality and spirit of teamwork. A *sine qua non* of successful teaching were habits of careful preparation, constructive and regular correction of pupils' work and a pervading ethos of encouragement. These good schools, moreover, all provided strong support for new entrants to the profession.

All ten refused to judge their success by examination results alone, but nevertheless all achieved and indeed aimed to achieve better than average results.

New premises, lavish equipment and liberal capitation allowances do not, by themselves, make a good school, but the lack of any of these things can, below a certain level, begin to hamper seriously the efforts of the most well-intentioned team of teachers. Some practical skills simply cannot be taught if there is no laboratory, workshop or equipment.

Schools vary widely in their relationships with the local community. The neighbourhood comprehensive may be set in a compact and close-knit community. I shall never forget a primary school in a deprived Manchester suburb which was so highly regarded by the locals that although vandalism was widespread, the school itself was never once damaged or burgled.

The ten good schools all enjoyed local esteem and their pupils had a proper pride in belonging to them. All ten schools made special arrangements to welcome visitors and parents. Information on pupils' progress was supplied regularly, both formally and informally. At least one of the schools also informed their pupils' former primary schools about their present progress. Indeed, I recall a Lincolnshire grammar school whose catchment area contained 57 primary schools. At the end of each pupil's first year, the headmistress sent a brief report to that pupil's former school. Four or five years later she sent news of each pupil's O Level and CSE results and whether they had got a job or were staying on into the sixth form. Moreover, the information was always presented as a kind of celebration of what 'we between us, secondary and primary schools, have managed to help this child achieve'. Needless to say the effort was greatly appreciated and amply repaid by cooperation from those primary schools.

The ten good schools, between them, made other contributions to the community. Some of them organised specific services for the community, notably with play groups, sick people and homebound aged. Others shared their premises with adult classes, dramatic societies, musical groups and other clubs. A few of the schools had developed international contacts and tapped into a wider community through exchange visits. All schools valued the Careers Advisory Service and saw careers guidance as an accepted part of pastoral care.

Finally, all ten schools, though widely varied in size, location and emphasis, had in common effective leadership and a 'climate' conducive to growth. All saw themselves as places designed for learning and all laid emphasis upon consultation and teamwork. Above everything else, each was led by a headteacher of energy, imagination and vision tempered by reality.

The importance of leadership has been emphasised time and again. It was noted as crucial in HMI's survey of schools which catered well for gifted pupils. It has been exhaustively researched by Professor J. Feldhusen of Purdue University, Dr E. Landau of Tel Aviv, Dr D. Sisk of Florida, Dr J. Cawood of Stellenbosch and Dr J. Burns. At the end of the 1970s it was a major consideration in a state-wide survey of 'school climate' which was carried out in the Commonwealth of Massachusetts.

Problems

Since the decision to publish HM inspectors' reports, the contents and procedures have themselves been subject to criticism by others. Indeed, HMI have always been self-critical and in search of improved ways to assess and report upon schools.

Various experiments have been tried. For a very brief period in the late 1960s and early 1970s some 'agreed reports' were produced, the texts of which were scrutinised and sometimes modified and finally agreed between the reporting HMIs and the headteachers of the schools concerned. On the face of it a democratic and fair procedure, this soon broke down in the case of poor schools and critical reports where agreement proved impossible. Ever since, HMI reports have been written by HMI alone following a full verbal account to the headteacher and governors of what the report would contain when later published.

There have also been other experiments with the length and format of full inspections including 'dipsticks' and 'short' inspections in which a less detailed assessment of the school is made.

The criticisms of HMI procedures have, however, seldom concerned the overall fairness or thoroughness of their reports, but have been directed at the objectivity of judgement of examination results and personal development of pupils.

Ever since the setting up of the APU at the DES in the early 1970s, there has been an increasing drive towards accountability and sharp assessment. The new Education Bill calls for the testing of all pupils at 7, 11, 14 and 16. Someone at some point must therefore be prepared to state and argue convincingly whether or not any given test result or school assessment is *satisfactory* or 'up to standard'.

In past reports HMI have often tolerantly noted that public examination results were 'encouraging' or 'acceptable' without offering any detailed analysis or basis of statistical comparison. This will not do in the colder late 1980s and 1990s.

Moreover, is it acceptable or even moral to apply different criteria to schools with very different social, economic and geographical backgrounds? It may well represent a heroic achievement for a poor, deprived, northern inner city school to get 50 per cent of its pupils through five GCSE subjects. The self-same outcome from an affluent, high employment, southern home county school would probably raise more than eyebrows. Are both results 'satisfactory'? Is the first 50 per cent 'excellent' and the second 50 per cent 'disappointing'? Should there be any subjective comment or judgement at all?

Various attempt have been made to overcome the problem. In California in 1978, state-wide assessment scores from the schools were carefully weighted or 'corrected' for such social and educational disadvantage factors as unemployment rate, proportion of one-parent families, ethnic mix and socio-economic status of the school board area. In the example above the first 50 per cent would be increased, the second diminished.

The ILEA devised what it called a 'performance score' for comparing the academic performances of its secondary schools. These performance scores were in essence raw scores weighted by social factors thought likely to affect them.

An even more difficult problem arises in judging personal development or 'school climate' when we do not even have 'raw scores' of any kind to manipulate. At present, HMI reports pay proper attention to such school 'outputs' but assessment, if it is hard enough to be so called, is still descriptive and highly subjective. However, much thought is being given to the matter.

Independent schools

All independent schools in England and Wales are subject to the 1944 Act and open to inspection. Before a school can even open for business it must obtain provisional registration. When it has been in operation for a short time an HMI visit is arranged and the school is assessed for full registration purposes. If registration is granted the school may continue. If it fails to meet the requirements, registration may be delayed until deficiencies are resolved, or the establishment may simply have to close.

Until Mrs Shirley Williams was Secretary of State for Education and Science, it was also possible for independent schools to seek 'recognition' by the DES. This higher status entailed a full inspection of the school and a rather more demanding set of criteria than those for registration alone. Recognition status was sought after and valued and usually proclaimed in independent school prospectuses.

Mrs Williams abolished recognition status and so the Independent

Schools Joint Council (ISJC) decided to set up its own Accreditation and Review Committee and organised, under a former divisional HM inspector, Mr P Burns, a system of accreditation visits to independent schools throughout the country. These visits were, and indeed are, led by retired HMIs and staffed by experienced independent school headteachers. The procedures are similar to those of a full HMI visitation. Work is scrutinised, lessons are visited, schemes of work, timetables, premises, resources, results and achievements are all examined and a report is produced. These reports are not published and, being intended solely for the ISJC, the relevant Association and the school itself, need not contain so much factual, descriptive detail as a published HMI report. They do, however, contain as much if not more candid comment and assessment.

Moreover, when an institution previously inspected and accredited suffers a change of headteacher, a review visit is arranged to ensure that former accreditation standards have been maintained.

Performance indicators

The information available to professionals is not normally available to others interested in school quality. Moreover, the regular detailed assessment of schools, whether by HMI, local inspectors or schools themselves, is a very expensive and time-consuming procedure. On the other hand, to base an assessment of a school purely upon its GCSE results, or the chicness of its uniform, or the behaviour of its pupils at local bus stops can be misleading.

Is there some short list of 'symptoms', 'characteristics' or 'indicators' which are generally associated with schools whose detailed bills of health are generally satisfactory? The ILEA Junior Survey described on page 51 produced such a list. Is there a more generalised and simpler set of indicators for schools of all kinds?

The *London Evening Standard* of 31 May 1988 and the *Observer* of 5 June 1988 both carried details of a DES statistical enquiry which is being pursued in eight of the 104 LEAs. Apart from examination results the following ten factors were also said to be of possible key significance and are under examination in this survey:

- Teacher turnover.
- Book and library provision.
- Support for pupils of poor basic attainment.
- Teacher expectation.
- Teacher-pupil contact time.

- Standards of attainment at 14.
- Whether homework is set and done.
- Pupil attendance and behaviour at school.
- Pupil participation in sport and extra-curricular activity.
- Views of local employers.

A different procedure known as Data Envelopment Analysis, currently under development by private management consultants, is researching the possibility of using such 'indicators' as pupil attendance records (at least 85 per cent of pupils turning up for lessons in winter months), voluntary option for subjects outside the National Curriculum (at least 90 per cent), good behaviour and appearance at the school gates (by at least 90 per cent), success in leavers getting jobs (as opposed to university places), and locally canvassed public opinion.

A few local authorities, including the ILEA and Croydon, have been trying to pinpoint similar indicators which will be useful to governing bodies with their increased responsibilities and even to the general public.

The teachers' professional associations, however, are understandably wary of short cuts to instant judgements on schools. Some have already insisted that any assessment of a school must take account of pupils' home backgrounds and related social and economic factors.

Can schools assess themselves?

No outsider, even a tenacious and diligent inspector, can possibly know as much about a school as its own teachers and pupils. Of course, any one pupil will only really know about her own class and any one teacher will probably know most about his own subject department, but taken together this in-house store of knowledge and self-critical perceptions ought to make it possible for schools to move in the direction of self-regulation if only this intelligence can be organised, reconciled, moderated and distilled. After all, any headteachers worth their salt will aim to make their pupils independent and capable of running their own lives and controlling their own behaviour.

So why should maintained schools not become self-regulating and autonomous in the same way that their fellow institutions in the independent sector are going? What are the bars and caveats? Are we even planning for this to happen? Other professionals such as doctors, social service workers and careers advisers manage their own affairs. Why not teachers?

It is, and always has been, my view that external inspection must ultimately give way to professional self-assessment and self-regulation.

The first-class teacher is the one whose pupils eventually no longer need his or her help. The successful parent is the one who rears his or her child to full independence. By analogy it must be one of the long-term aims of HM Inspectorate to so train and inform those who run the system that eventually they can monitor it efficiently themselves.

A heartening number of enterprising attempts at self-evaluation have been made. *Keeping the School under Review*, a method of self-assessment for schools devised by the ILEA Inspectorate and published by the ILEA in 1983, offers to primary and secondary schools and colleges of further education respectively long lists of questions that teachers might ask themselves about key aspects of their work. For primary schools these clutches of questions involve: The Children, Parental and Community Involvement, Managers, Programmes (Schemes) of Work or Guidelines, Class Organisation, Staffing, Simple Statistics, General Environment, Action, Questions for the head-teacher to ask him or herself and Questions for the individual teacher to ask him or herself. As a footnote, 'acid test' questions include (1) Would I recommend a colleague to apply for a post in the school? (2) Would I recommend the school to friends for their children?

The secondary school groups of questions naturally reflect the organisation of the institution and include such headings as Simple Statistics, School Environment, Resources, Decision-making and Communications, Staff, Pupils, Parental and Community Links, Arrangements for Learning, Departmental (or faculty) Self-Assessment, Questions for the headteacher to ask him or herself and Questions for the individual teacher to ask him or herself.

Many ILEA schools have worked conscientiously through this exercise and discussed their own findings and self-assessments with their own ILEA inspectors. The actual process concentrated the mind splendidly, offered valuable inservice training to new teachers and, although time-consuming, was generally seen as worthwhile. It was not always easy to synthesise the mountains of individual question responses, however objective and candid, into a global judgement about the school as a whole.

This ILEA procedure, which started in 1977, was adopted, after a few years, in modified form by Oxfordshire LEA.

Self-assessment of individual achievement

Oxfordshire has also developed a unique initiative entitled the Oxfordshire Certificate of Educational Achievement (OCEA).

Developed by a consortium of local authorities and the Oxford Delegacy for Local Examinations, OCEA is not just a piece of paper but a kind of dossier or profile resulting from continuous assessment.

The idea started in the modern languages field with graded assessments to show progress, but now extends to English and science. Ultimately, one assumes, it will cover all subjects of the curriculum.

The OCEA comprises a list of skills acquired, examination certificates gained and a summary of achievements written by each pupil, including out of school achievements. The system thus involves the pupils in their own learning and self-assessment, and the OCEA criteria have considerably affected classroom organisation and teaching methods.

For example, in English there is emphasis upon oral skills and group discussion. Each pupil is thus assessed on his or her ability to state an opinion or argue a case and also on the ability to listen and follow the contributions of others. In science the emphasis is on planning experiments, organising work, observing and performing. So the overall emphasis is much more upon what pupils can *do* than what they do not know or can not do.

So far the scheme is being tried in Coventry, Leicestershire, Oxfordshire and Somerset.

A rather similar self-assessment-cum-profiling initiative operates in Harrow. The Harrow Record of Achievement offers a record of the students' activities, achievements and potential in school and beyond up to the age of 16. It presently relates mainly to the last two years of compulsory education in certain pilot schools and contains a Student Statement, covering personal qualities, interests, courses taken and skills developed, experience of work and future plans; and a School Statement.

The Student Statement is written by the student with help from his or her personal tutor; the School Statement is written by the school but shown to the student before its final form is approved and issued. Each record is signed by the Chairman of the School's Validations Board, the Chairman of the Local Authorities Accrediting Board (currently the author) and the Chairman of the Accrediting Council for Education (currently Mr Peter Newson). The record is handsomely produced in a grey folder large enough to contain other examination certificates and relevant documents.

In the first year's run some anticipated difficulties emerged but not nearly so prominently as feared. For example, there *was* a tendency to emphasise the positive and play down the negative although, curiously, some of the students were more candid about their own shortcomings than the staff were about the pupils. Indeed, I found the 'ring of truth' in some of the students' self-assessments more appealing than the carefully laundered school prose with its scope for 'between the lines' guesswork and possible misinterpretation.

The whole process did throw a considerable extra work load on staff, but they bore it bravely and contributed greatly to the success of the first run. How they will cope with the further burdens imposed by teacher assessment, course work organisation, moderation demands of GCSE, and the National Curriculum is an open question.

Thirdly, the fear that admission tutors in colleges of further education and employers would ignore the profile and look only at the examination certificates was exaggerated; feedback was encouraging and positive.

In-school testing

The most traditional mode of 'self-assessment' used by schools includes regular testing, year exams and reports to parents.

To read the Secretary of State's plans for testing all pupils in all subjects at 7, 11, 14 and 16, the person in the street might be forgiven for thinking that schools do not already test their pupils. In fact in *Testing Children* (Heinemann 1983) by C Gipps it was claimed that by 1981 at least 79 per cent of all LEAs had some or other programme of testing primary school pupils; 12 per cent left decisions about testing to the schools themselves. Reading has always been the most commonly tested skill and by 1981 70 per cent of LEAs were using a specific reading test with at least one age group – while 35 per cent were testing two or three age groups, usually 7-, 8- or 11-year-olds. Mathematics testing occurred in only about 40 per cent of all LEAs, and then at 11 years, although most individual schools did, and still do, test children in this subject.

This practice has increased since 1981 and the latest estimates suggest that 90 per cent of primary schools test reading in some way or other, while 70 per cent test mathematics. The range of tests from NFER, Nelson and other publishers has increased to meet this need.

The surge of testing has occurred in the wake of the national APU surveys which themselves generated item banks of test material in language, mathematics, modern languages and science. The question of national assessment will be discussed in the next chapter, but meanwhile it must be obvious that a great deal of self-assessment through testing, self-questioning and other means already occurs.

The role of pupils, parents and governors

We have already seen that in some schools pupils play a significant part in assessing the work that goes on.

Most governing bodies now contain parent representatives and it is mainly through these that a formal parental role in school assessment operates.

For although many schools have active parents' associations and although most parents are very concerned about the quality of their children's schools, parents as a body are seldom involved in any formal evaluation of them. Also it should not be forgotten that, as the 1988 *Sunday Times*/Mori poll showed, 78 per cent of Britain's parents are satisfied with their children's education. In its own 1988 survey, the ILEA showed that 75 per cent of its parents are similarly happy.

Not content with this, a few schools have pioneered courses on education for parents or parenthood with a view to encouraging a more active and constructively critical interest.

School governors, however, under the 1986 Education Act which took on many of the Taylor Committee recommendations, will have a more demanding and significant role to play than formerly. They have a right to see all curriculum documents and syllabuses and their recorded deliberations must be open to the public. However, they need to be trained and indeed some LEAs have already run some very good courses and produced some useful learning packs for the purpose.

Governors must be careful about confidential items but are expected to be helpfully critical about the achievements and learning outcomes of the schools they manage.

The 1988 Education Reform Act adds to these powers giving governors more responsibility for financial management and staff appointments and – a much publicised issue – will give them powers to initiate change to 'government maintained' status – ie to 'opt out' of LEA control – the ultimate assessment sanction.

Chapter 4

Improving the School

Using the assessment

Action or *deliberate* inaction should always follow assessment. Ideally, this is a continuous process, the daily surveillance of a child's or class's work feeding the teacher messages not only about the child's or the class's progress but about the effectiveness of his or her own teaching or appropriateness of the material used.

However, assuming that a school has undergone some more extensive inspection, review or even self-assessment, the question 'What next?' must arise.

HM inspections of maintained schools

The procedure following a full inspection by HMIs is clearly prescribed:

1. At the end of the week of the inspection or survey, each inspector gives the headteacher a careful assessment of the work he or she has seen.

   Each inspector will probably also have spoken to the individual teachers seen and to the head of department responsible for that subject. Indeed, it is not unusual for a full departmental discussion with the HMI concerned to take place.

   By way of conclusion, the leader of the inspection team, or 'reporting inspector', will summarise the overall broad judgement of the team and try to boil down their host of individual comments and assessments into a handful of major issues about the school as a whole.

   Some of these will be strengths and growth points which the school may nurture; others may be concerned with weaknesses which require consideration and planned improvement.

2. In the case of a full inspection (although not for isolated short visits), the governing body of the school is invited to meet the reporting HMI fairly soon afterwards.

   On this occasion (the invitation is nearly always accepted) the governors are given a brief oral account of the main issues which are likely to appear in the published report. The headteacher is always present and the governors are able to ask questions, comment on and even query the findings. Very occasionally, points of judgement by HMIs have been disputed and modifications accepted. After all, the inspectors have usually only been in the school for a week at most whereas governors have sometimes been associated with and made themselves knowledgeable about and helpful to the school over a very long period. This meeting is accordingly seen as an important *part of*, rather than adjunct to, the full inspection process.

3. The actual production of an HMI report can be a lengthy process. The text must be agreed by all those who worked on the inspection team. It must then be vetted by the divisional or territorial staff inspector, the phase staff inspector and by subject staff inspectors. If controversial, it may even have to run the gamut of chief inspectors. This can be a lengthy process, at best six months but sometimes over a year. Eventually the published text emerges and is sent simultaneously to the headteacher and the governing body.

   Most schools set about meeting any criticism made as soon as the inspection is over and it is not uncommon to find that when the published report arrives many of the problems have already been tackled.

4. Six months or so after the publication of an HMI report, the DES will write to the LEA (or, if an independent school, the governors) noting the major points raised in the report, and enquiring what action has been taken.

LEA inspections of maintained schools

Many large LEAs have their own teams of inspectors or advisors whose roles vary and are determined not by the DES but by the LEA itself.

In some authorities that role has been strongly advisory with an emphasis upon support, inservice training and inspirational leadership. In others the role has been more inspectorial with an emphasis upon assessment.

LEA inspections of schools, where they occur, follow broadly the pattern of HMI inspections, but reports are not published and the follow-up action is purely a matter for the local authority, its advisers and the school, the DES not being involved.

Two authorities are particularly worthy of note. The ILEA, due to be disbanded in 1989, maintained a powerful, highly professional and generously resourced inspectorate who organised regular inspections of schools. They also participated in a system of 'quinquennial reviews' whereby selected schools conducted detailed self-assessments with some 'external' advice and moderation from the local ILEA inspector.

The ILEA also used the considerable expertise of its research department to ensure that the 'ability profile' of a school and local social factors were taken into full account when assessing the achievement of an institution.

Croydon LEA has also developed unusual inspection procedures and very thorough assessment practices in its schools. Since 1986 it has separated the function of advising, supporting and inservice training from that of 'evaluating' and reporting upon the quality of the consequent work. Thus, the prime function of Croydon's inspectorate is to assess the quality of education provided in the borough's schools, and inspections of primary schools are to occur, for example, every five years.

The declared aims of Croydon's inspections are to improve quality, provide information upon which LEA policy can be based, allow open discussion of the criteria employed and ensure that the processes of inspection are clearly understood. The authority has also made clear that those responsible for inspection will always have had personal experience of teaching and organising the work they are inspecting.

HMI and LEA inspectors

In 1988 Sir David Hancock, the Permanent Secretary at the DES, redefined the role of local inspectors and advisors once the Education Reform Bill becomes law. He called for closer cooperation between local inspectors and HMIs but insisted that their roles will be 'clearly differentiated' and that they would maintain their 'independent reporting lines'. He did not dismiss the continuing need for local inspectorate support and advice but he did feel that the Croydon-type trend was desirable and inevitable, within the obligations of the Bill, and that the inspection and reporting function of LEA inspectors would need to be given an even higher profile and priority.

This added up to more work and a necessary expansion in the local inspectorate service and he announced that the government intended to institute a new five-year ESG (Education Support Grant) which would increase the force by 10 per cent.

Independent schools

Independent schools are not subject to many of the provisions of the 1988 Education Reform Act and will not be obliged to follow or adopt the National Curriculum. This will clearly make sense for the specialist music and ballet schools, but the signs are that many independent schools will consider very carefully before they diverge too far from what will become a new curriculum entitlement for 94 per cent of the nation's children.

There will, therefore, be less need to support and monitor changes in independent schools and, although these schools are subject to inspection by HMI (but not local inspectors), and indeed are sometimes fully inspected, the onus of inspectorial work is likely to concern mainly the maintained schools.

Seeing this trend grow over recent years, the ISJC, set up its own Accreditation, Review and Consultancy Service as we saw in Chapter 3. Its current director, Mr TWF Allan, organises an inspection programme and maintains a flow of inspection reports to the independent school organisations, The Incorporated Association of Preparatory Schools, The Society of Headmasters of Independent Schools, and the Independent Schools' Association Incorporated. These are written by retired HMIs who lead the visits and they are produced within a month or two of the visit. They are not published, but are made available to the headteachers and staff, governing bodies and professional associations of the schools concerned. Follow-up and remedial action is pursued as enthusiastically as in the state sector – sometimes more so.

Follow-up action

Consequential action, whether from an HMI, LEA or ISJC report, often falls into three different categories: short-, medium- and long-term issues.

SHORT-TERM ISSUES

These are usually of a material nature. For example, the absence of a safety lock on the pottery kiln, a loose fire escape handrail, a slippery floor surface round a lathe, the undue proximity of a domestic science room power point and water supply, etc can all be rectified swiftly.

Sometimes a practice or lack of it is in question. In one school young pupils arrived, deposited their bags and went straight to assembly. It was suggested that a five-minute form tutor period would give coherence and form spirit and make it possible to despatch items of business which otherwise punctuated the day. Moreover, the incidence of tardiness and truancy might be reduced. The headteacher introduced such a tutor session overnight and subsequently retained it, so successful did it prove.

Deficiencies of books, particularly reference books or small items of equipment glaringly obvious to the onlooker but blissfully managed without by the school, can often be quickly procured.

One primary school possessed no encyclopaedias. When the lack of these, library atlases and other useful reference books was noted, they were purchased the day after the inspection. Likewise, a timesaving electronic scientific balance was acquired within a few weeks of the inspector's visit.

Perhaps the most dramatic short-term improvement, although hardly a 'small item', occurred after my first ever country primary school full inspection. During torrential rain water began to drip through in several places in the classroom where I was watching a lesson. Accustomed to this interruption the teacher quickly produced plastic buckets, moved a few desks and resumed her lesson. 'It's been like this for years,' she said. In my report I pulled few punches in my description of the school buildings and the roof in particular. Imagine my satisfaction when, driving past three weeks later, I noticed that this 1842 building had at last acquired a new twentieth-century hat!

MEDIUM-TERM ISSUES

Not all deficiencies are so easily rectified. Staff cannot be engaged at less than a term's notice so where the staffing structure of a school is unbalanced or where, say, a drama tutor has left and not been replaced, the problem can usually not be solved in less than a term or two.

Inservice training is also a medium-term issue. I recall a young member of staff who had been detailed to introduce computer studies. With little expertise but with the best will in the world he was struggling to keep a page ahead of the class. He needed the opportunity for study, preparation and a proper inservice training course. Computer studies was unlikely to improve in that school within a term or two.

Sizeable building deficiencies also need longer-term planning. An independent preparatory school which applied for accreditation had to be refused on the grounds that it possessed no science laboratory or science room of any description. Science was taught out of books with the occasional nature ramble to add a dimension of practicality. It took the school a year to build a science laboratory and put its science teaching on to a practical experimental basis.

LONG-TERM ISSUES

A secondary school seldom has a full inspection more than once in ten years and so the full inspection report must take a fairly long-term view. Weaknesses of a major and serious nature require careful consideration by the headteacher and the governors. Possible remedies may entail lengthy staff discussion, external advice, a whole programme of inservice training, a radical restructuring of buildings or staff, or both, and major funding.

A few examples spring to mind. The amalgamation of two schools has sometimes been more of a paper exercise than a carefully planned, practical one. Thus, two very different schools just over a mile apart were placed under one headteacher. One had been a small, single sex secondary modern girls' school, the other a larger, traditional mixed grammar school. From the start there was an imbalance of boys and girls, an imbalance of laboratory, workshop and home economics provision, very unequal playing areas and a staff which was fragmented and tended to adhere to earlier loyalties.

The full inspection unearthed a host of problems requiring long-term planning and some which appeared intractable. For example, I calculated that the groups of children who had to walk regularly between the schools in order to use immovable specialist facilities covered altogether each year a distance greater than that between the earth and the moon – a waste of time and shoe leather to say the least. Thus, there were major problems of attitude, philosophy, organisation and rebuilding whose solution took years to accomplish.

Such demands are not unusual. I recall a streamed school faced with a new headteacher's determination to introduce mixed ability grouping throughout before any curriculum planning or staff inset had taken place.

Another Midlands school, over a short period of demographic upheaval, changed from an all-white establishment into one where West Indian and Asian youngsters outnumbered the remainder. Here the headteacher and his unchanged staff were having to cope with major problems of language, custom, religious belief, attitude to learning and parental bewilderment. None of these proved short- or even medium-term difficulties.

Facing the problems: focusing and prioritising

Faced with an assessment which has pinpointed several weaknesses and matters requiring attention, the headteacher and the staff must plan their response. It is seldom possible to tackle everything at once. There is never sufficient time, money and resources. Indeed, even if there were, and frantic changes were made in every area criticised, one could never isolate the effects of each initiative to decide whether it had worked.

Clearly small, short-term problems which involve safety practices and/or modest expenditure can and should be dealt with immediately.

Medium-term issues can usually be put in hand – a post advertised, an architect consulted, a small working party set up, and so on.

The long-term major issues together pose two main questions. (1) Is any one of these issues *primus inter pares*, of priority over all others? (2) Is a focused attack by all staff on this issue feasible?

Sometimes the priority is determined by external factors. In 1988 the enforced introduction of GCSE examinations pre-empted all other efforts in schools. However unprepared or unwilling, schools simply had to gear themselves to the new demands and procedures of the new examinations.

In September 1989 when the Education Reform Bill becomes law, schools will simply have to start teaching the new National Curriculum. The law and the timing will determine the priorities.

The choice is not always so sharp. I recall a middle school which was criticised on three main counts: the poor discipline, sloppy marking and notable weaknesses in the teaching and learning of reading skills. In the event the staff, with a new headteacher, decided to focus on these issues *in turn*. They drew up three different scenarios. In the end they decided to tackle the reading problem across the whole staff and curriculum. Every teacher became a teacher of English in his or her own subject. The interest and support of parents was invoked, a new language scheme was devised and the library and drama activities were both broadened and extended.

The interesting outcome, foreseen by some of those who had favoured this priority, was that the marking *automatically* become more thorough, systematic and supportive. Moreover, this newly imposed discipline of learning seemed to spill over beneficially into the general morale and discipline of the school.

In this case an assault upon the particular seemed to produce beneficial spin-offs of a more generalised nature, but the reverse policy can also work. In another, not dissimilar, case a school staff planned a focused attack upon a broad cross-curricular deficiency in record-keeping. By developing their own records of achievement procedure, agreed and operated by all departments, some earlier weaknesses in individual subjects began to disappear.

Much depends upon the 'critical path analysis' of 'what to tackle first' which must follow any major assessment. Successive focusing upon an agreed order of priorities requires teamwork, sacrifice, very professional attitudes and strong, inspired leadership. One department may have to sacrifice some of its allowance or limelight in favour of another, and await its turn. In the long run, however, this is the best response to a school assessment.

Chapter 5

The Use and Abuse of School Assessments

In Chapter 4 we looked at ways of making use of careful assessments of schools. The approach was idealistic. The assessments were assumed to have been thorough and constructive. It was also assumed that the school accepted as fair the judgements made and was disposed to respond positively to most if not all of them.

My own experience is that this is frequently, indeed *usually*, the case. Teachers and inspectors (who have nearly all been successful teachers themselves) are professional people generally united in their desire to do their best for the children they directly or indirectly serve.

Occasionally, of course, there are disagreements and upsets and cases of injured pride. I can think of at least one department whose head was completely at loggerheads with the visiting inspector. They differed fundamentally over aims, objectives, syllabus and methodology, and both held their ground. When the report was finally issued the disputed section on English was duly ignored.

There have also been cases of disagreement over the overall judgement of a whole school – and indeed of a whole authority. There was, for example, an orthodox Jewish school in London whose curriculum was predominantly religious and whose secular provision was deemed to fall below DES requirements. The Department took the school to a legal tribunal but lost the case. There have also been cases where, for example, the seemingly overliberal/excessively democratic management of a school has incurred parental disquiet and, subsequently, inspectorial criticism which has fallen on deaf ears. Ethnic and/or multi-racial issues have also divided parents and whole communities in at least two celebrated cases.

In recent years, the DES has even mounted whole LEA inspections and in at least one of these, fundamental differences of values and ideology have made it difficult to reach agreement about strengths and weaknesses and necessary action.

None of these cases could be described as an *abuse* of school assessment. Limited use, yes, but not abuse. Abuse arises all too frequently from mischievous, partial, partisan reporting. There are those who will not see what is placed under their noses. There are politicians or politically motivated people whose dogma does not allow them to see any good in types of schools of which they disapprove. In the education debate which has been rumbling on ever since Mr Callaghan's 'Ruskin Speech', there have been, on the one hand, those on the right who would almost by definition condemn a school simply because it was comprehensive. At the other extreme, left-wing attitudes to independent schools and assisted places in them blind the holders of these views to the very real areas of excellence to be found in this sector.

Misrepresentation can take many forms. When a school report has been leaked into unsympathetic hands, it is easy to publish only critical passages and to ignore commendatory ones. Worse, a passage, instead of being quoted, may be paraphrased, garbled or distorted so as to produce a blacker (or whiter) picture.

Sometimes, it is clear that a criticism or suggestion has been completely misunderstood and, accordingly, misconstrued by a reporter. In rare cases, hearsay, unsubstantiated criticisms or even fabricated 'evidence' have been spread and even published in order to denigrate a school.

Open reporting

Sir Keith Joseph, a somewhat maligned but scrupulous former Secretary of State for Education, insisted upon scrutinising all the available evidence before making his decisions. In spite of his party views he would not countenance the kind of dishonest reportage described above and he realised that one way to discourage poisoned leakage was to publish all HMI reports openly.

There had always been a rubric insisting that HMI should be quoted in full, or not at all, but Sir Keith made copies of all HMI reports publicly available from the DES Publications Despatch Centre at Honeypot Lane, Stanmore, Middlesex. So at least the person in the street could read for him or herself the whole assessment upon any school which had been inspected by HMI.

The ILEA followed suit but most other LEAs issue LEA assessments to individual schools and their governing bodies in confidence. The same procedure is followed by the ISJC Accreditation, Review and Consultancy Service. In these cases no other procedure is feasible on grounds of expense alone.

It does, however, leave open the whole question of reporting school assessments.

The case against

There are still those who feel that the whole process should be confidential. Why, they say, should dirty washing be washed in public? After all, there are no publicly produced assessments or critiques of local social service departments, or indeed other local transport, health or refuse services. So why parade a school's shortcomings before the public gaze?

The cost of open reporting is also heavy. Where a school's inspection hits the headlines there is a great demand for free copies of the report. In one case, the school claimed, every parent sent for a free copy of the report! On the other hand, where the inspection/reporting procedure is – as is more usual – a low-key, professional affair, there are few requests for copies of the published report.

Timing is also a germane issue. The lengthy scrutinising process to which HMI draft reports are subjected means that a period of time of at least six months and, in exceptional cases, up to two years may elapse between the inspection and the publication of the report. By the time the report hits the headlines it can be well out of date. The short- and medium-term problems may well have been dealt with. Not infrequently, the staff, including the headteacher, and even the status of the school may have changed. The scent is cold, the assessment half forgotten. However, this does not always stop mischievous reporters from scratching old sores.

Confidentiality

The issue of confidentiality affects all assessments and reporting. Your doctor is prevented by the Hippocratic Oath from discussing his or her assessment of your medical condition with other patients. Lately the principle has come under pressure from such questions as:

Shouldn't parents know if contraceptive pills, VD treatment or potentially addictive drugs are being prescribed for dependent children?

Shouldn't a spouse have the right to know whether her or his partner has been diagnosed as suffering from, or carrying, the AIDS virus or some other sexually transmitted disease?

Similar questions surround education. Should a school assessment be made public to those not directly concerned? Clearly, there is a strong case for governors, headteachers and staff to have access to the report. There is even a case for local employers and receiving colleges to see it. Parents should know about it through their representative governor on the school board. But is it really anyone else's business?

After all, one would not send Jimmy Smith's end of term report, or public examination results, to Mary Brown's parents. One would not publish *internal* reports and examination results in the local press. So why should whole-school assessments be open to public gaze and unsympathetic or ill-informed censure? The answer given is that the public pay the rates – that those who pay the piper should call the tune. But if this argument is valid, why is it not applied elsewhere?

Paradoxically, open reporting has, in the event, done more good than harm. It has seldom led to major disagreement and it has made the public more aware of their education system and more informed about the most expensive service on their rate bills.

Future trends

The Freedom of Information Act makes it even more incumbent upon all inspectors, HMI or local authority, to avoid all personal comment about individual teachers, not only in their reports but also in their notes and files. What matters is the work, the quality of education, the intangible outcomes.

It is not always easy to avoid personal comment by implication. In a small school where only one teacher is responsible for a given subject, comment upon that area of work is bound to reflect directly upon that teacher. Even where personal comment is not published or implied, the notebooks and file drafts continue in existence and these may contain inaccuracies.

Within the last two years many DES and HMI offices have been equipped with computer terminals and data storage systems. It is now possible for a middle management HMI to call up written and statistical data obtained during the last inspection. This is clearly a powerful management tool. Provided the information is up to date, factually correct and the assessments made are well based, it should be possible to create or change policy in a rapid, sensitive and fine-tuned way.

It should also be possible to collate information rapidly and to obtain, in a short time, the current or at best latest local or even national picture of, say, attainment records in secondary schools, computer usage in primary schools, classics in maintained sixth forms. That picture can only be as good as the classroom, face-to-face assessment upon which it is based.

Those who assess schools are in a very responsible and privileged position. It is easier to see faults in others than in oneself. It is easy to place too much reliance upon hearsay. It is easy to assume that what is seen on a fleeting visit is typical and to underestimate the effect of one's own presence upon the situation one is examining. Memories fade and what we say one day, and describe in writing a week later, may well carry quite different messages.

In spite of all this the process at best is invaluable. It is only through careful, wise and humane continuous assessment and self-assessment that the nation's schools will continue to improve and help our growing children – our seedcorn – as much as they might.

Chapter 6

Assessing Special Kinds of Schools

To any happy pupil his or her own school is 'special'. There are also a number of schools which by the articles of government, by intention or by happy accident become known for outstanding success or special expertise in some particular area of the curriculum. Thus, we find maintained secondary schools which are known for their success in mathematics, drama or art but which otherwise offer a broad, sound education. To such schools the criteria of assessment differ little from those discussed earlier in this book although the area of expertise might well attract more interest or more detailed scrutiny from a visiting team of inspectors than would usually be the case.

There are also many denominational schools and some Jewish schools within the maintained sector. Here again, visiting professionals would assess the work of such schools in much the same way as they would any other maintained schools, but the parents' basis of judgement of such schools might be different. For the orthodox Jewish or the devout Catholic parent, the most important aspect of the school might well be the quality of its religious life and ethos and the training it offers. Indeed, there are those who would sacrifice quality in other aspects of the school, in its buildings, location, resources or organisation even, provided the essential spiritual component was strong and effective. I would not presume to suggest a checklist for assessing this dimension systematically but such parents most definitely apply their own.

The official view would undoubtedly be that in all such schools the secular education and the material circumstances should meet the same criteria that are applied to other schools.

There are, however, two broad classes of schools which need to be looked at in a rather different fashion: schools for handicapped pupils and schools for the performing arts.

Schools for handicapped pupils

Until the Warnock Committee produced its report there had existed a number of special schools for various physical and intellectual handicaps. We had schools for the blind, the deaf, the delicate, the severely subnormal and the educationally subnormal. There was also provision for children with cerebral palsy, epileptics and a variety of other severely handicapping conditions. In these schools could also be found those with partial sight, partial hearing and multiple handicaps.

The parents of such pupils had little choice. If your child is deaf, he or she must simply go to *the* nearest school for the deaf.

Of course this made it all the more important that such schools were up to scratch. And indeed, as far as HM Inspectorate was concerned, these highly specialised institutions were regularly visited by inspectors with specialist expertise in these fields. In 1983 the ILEA produced in its Learning Materials Service, *Keeping the School under Review*, a document on the special school. The broad structure of this assessment schedule was similar to that for secondary schools. In other words, due regard was paid to pupils and staff, curriculum, organisation, observation and recording and to the building and material resources provided. Many of the questions echoed those that one would ask in a normal secondary or primary school. However, within the sections there were, as might be expected, questions related to the special functions of these schools.

On *children* it is clearly important to enquire very closely how they were assessed and came to be in the school. Are their handicaps accurately diagnosed and recorded and do they have links with specialist medical, social and perhaps psychological services outside the school?

Many of them have to travel long distances and so the questions of their waking day, meal timing and transport need to be checked. I shall never forget, in my early days in the Inspectorate, discovering a blue bus that meandered round scattered villages picking up pupils for the special school in a nearby town. The earliest 11-year-old traveller was picked up at a country lane end, rain or shine, at 7.30 am each morning and was dropped there at 5.30 pm every evening. He told me he did not mind the life but I failed to see the educational value of so much travel and wasted time. Not long after, the authority opened a special unit in the local comprehensive school so that such children could at least go to school with their contemporaries.

Reverting to special schools, it is also necessary to assess the qualifications and experience of the *staff* for their roles. One wise chief education officer of my acquaintance would never appoint teachers to special schools direct from college even when they had undertaken an extra course in their intended specialism. He was anxious that every new teacher should learn the standards of which normal children are capable; it is all too easy to feel sentimental about, and expect too little of, handicapped children. The issue of expectation is one of the most important to look for in the work and teaching of a special school.

Buildings and *equipment* feature strongly in specialised schools. Buildings often require a greater measure of security, lifts and/or stair lifts and ramps for wheelchairs. Sometimes a bath is necessary for hydrotherapy and properly equipped spaces for other physiotherapeutic purposes. Floor covering, heating, seating, working and storage facilities are also important.

In recent years many computer programmes, modified keyboards and other electronic and technological aids have been devised to facilitate learning for the handicapped. Any proper assessment of a special school must include a comprehensive review of such facilities.

Curriculum and *organisation* are often very different in a special school. Language acquisition for a profoundly deaf or autistic child may involve such a struggle in itself that the learning of another language would be quite out of the question. Likewise some of the skills of dexterity, coordination and balance taught to normal children in practical science, handicrafts and PE would be beyond some handicapped pupils.

Special schools are also usually much smaller than ordinary schools and it is common to find more individual and group work, indeed greater flexibility of organisation altogether, than might be seen in a large secondary school.

Inservice training necessary for special school teachers includes help with specialised skills and new techniques applicable to specific disabilities, but there is also a need for the kind of training and updating required by all teachers in the fields of GCSE assessment, profiling and so on.

Standards of work are closely related to the nature of the disability suffered. Even though severely *physically* handicapped, some children are capable of distinguished academic and aesthetic achievements, particularly where technological and electronic aids are available to help offset the physical limitations. Helen Keller, blind, deaf and dumb, nevertheless achieved fame and high achievement in academic fields. Indeed, the physically handicapped have even excelled in *physical* fields of endeavour: witness the New York and London Marathons and the

Paraplegic Olympics and the handicapped athletes who take part in them.

In the school or unit for the *educationally* subnormal it is not usual to find standards of work comparable with those in ordinary schools. But even here there is a surprising range of achievement and performance. Outstanding examples of good special school practice in recent years have taught us that there are real dangers in underexpectation. Most pupils, of all sorts and conditions, can often do better than we expect in some activity or other.

It is probably for this reason that the major trend since the publication of the Warnock Report has been to educate as many handicapped children as possible, not in special schools but in ordinary ones. Thus, for example, radio links have made it possible for hearing-impaired children to function quite normally in ordinary primary and secondary schools. Of course, other modifications to the schools have also been necessary.

Nowadays, only the severely handicapped who need highly specialised apparatus, methodology (eg Braille) and help are necessarily placed in special institutions.

Special school assessment must sometimes embrace the peculiar needs of *boarding schools*. Schools for the blind and the profoundly deaf are not numerous and some therefore admit pupils from a very wide catchment area. This often involves weekly or full-time residence. Naturally, all the criteria one would apply to any boarding school apply. Variety and quality of food, furnishing of dormitories, washing and toilet facilities, laundry, heating, lighting, sanatoria for illness, fire precautions, recreation rooms and so on must all reach acceptable standards, but in a boarding school for handicapped children additional criteria may apply. For example, feeding may be a more complex affair if children have cerebral palsy or are on special diets or require regular medication, pills with meals, etc.

In some schools furnishing and facilities may need to be supplemented with furniture, baths and WCs which are specially designed or adapted for specific handicaps. More extensive medical back-up is also likely to be necessary.

It is not the purpose of this chapter to provide a highly detailed schedule of questions that need to be addressed by a professional assessor but simply to indicate those factors which contribute to any overall school assessment.

The overriding aim of any school for any kind of physically or mentally handicapped child is that it should identify precisely the needs and potential strengths of that child and enable him or her to overcome that handicap as successfully as possible and to develop his or her gifts optimally.

Management, teaching methodology, pastoral care, premises, resources and staffing must all be arranged and geared to this purpose as effectively as possible.

Schools for the performing arts

MUSIC

Generally speaking these are schools which offer a strong bias towards music or dance education or, to a lesser extent, drama.

Some of these schools are highly specialised. The Yehudi Menuhin School at Stoke d'Abernon in Surrey, currently celebrating its 25th anniversary, has never had more than about 50 pupils, nearly all of whom board. They are selected personally by Sir Yehudi Menuhin for outstanding promise on the piano, violin or cello and they range in age from 8 to 18 and come from all over the world.

The Purcell School in Harrow on the Hill is more broadly based and although geared to producing concert performers, it admits woodwind and brass as well as string players, at least two of the former having won the Young Musician of the Year Award.

Chetham's School, Manchester, is a much larger school than either the Purcell or the Menuhin schools. It admits pupils on the basis of talent in any musical instrument and academic ability and has also produced some outstanding young performers. The headmaster follows every one of these young people with great care. Some fulfil their original promise beyond all expectations. Others develop strongly as expected and pursue careers of various kinds in music. A few lose their early shine and become more academic. These pupils are sometimes transferred to other schools whose aims correspond more to their developing strengths.

Wells Cathedral School began life as a grammar school with musical strengths and here musicians and non-musicians work side by side on rather different curricula.

Parents with a highly gifted musical youngster face a difficult dilemma. Is he or she *really* good enough to achieve a concert career or at least make a real success of music? If there is any doubt, might it not be better to stay in a pacey academic school and pursue music part-time? This was precisely the choice facing several parents of my acquaintance. Some took the plunge and sent their children to specialist music schools; others played safe.

The problem is exacerbated with gifted young string and keyboard players who need to be in a special school by the age of 8 if they are to have any hope of platform honours. Woodwind and brass players can make a later start on the road to mastery.

Given a strong commitment to specialist musical education, parents, as will be seen, are left with little choice. How do they decide which school? How do they assess the sprinkling of specialist schools? What criteria do they use?

As far as the non-musical components are concerned, all schools, whether specialist or not, must offer a broad, sound academic education. Although they can hardly be expected to offer as full a range of academic courses as a large comprehensive or top-class independent secondary school, they must provide a core of English, mathematics, science, humanities, art/craft and PE.

If maintained, they must offer the National Curriculum; if not, they should offer the core subjects and as many of the others as possible. They should be well housed and resourced for day and boarding purposes, and must provide the same pastoral support that would be deemed satisfactory in a maintained school.

But the specialist music school must offer much more than this. As far as the specialist curriculum is concerned one would expect to find the following:

1. good professional players and teachers of the instruments taught;
2. occasional supervision by a top-class exponent of the instrument;
3. opportunities for private practice from very early morning until late;
4. experience of chamber and orchestral music of all kinds;
5. opportunities to play to audiences of all kinds – fellow students, parents, other musicians, the general public, young children, elderly groups, hospices, etc. Musical performance is about communication in many different registers and being able to establish a rapport quickly; it requires, like pure technique, much practice;
6. opportunities to hear notable performers of one's own and other instruments;
7. opportunities for suitable physical exercise which is not likely to endanger the hands.

Alongside these must go tuition and experience in theory – score reading and analysis, arrangement, composing skills, etc. One bee in my own bonnet concerns *improvisation*. I have been privileged to hear many gifted young musicians play. Nearly always they were practising scales, arpeggios, fingering and bow techniques via exercises, or they were studying and learning a piece of music or yet another great work from the repertoire. The latter, of course, involves the exercise of creativity in that every performance should carry an element of personal interpretation, but all too rarely have I found young musicians improvising in the way that JS Bach must have improvised endlessly in his organ loft. Indeed, I have met some students who were so constipated by a stodgy diet of rigorous routine exercises that they did not know how to explore a theme or an idea on their own instrument.

Apart from all this, the specialist music school needs contacts of a kind that will help with the speedy repair, adjustment, loan and even purchase of instruments. At the career end, leavers will need very careful counselling about the next stage of their study or professional life.

Finally, on the purely domestic side, there are problems of diet and global air travel and communication with far-flung homes and parents which can tax any bursar.

In the end, the aims are very similar to those of the schools for the handicapped. Have talents been accurately assessed and the very utmost effective effort been made to develop them?

DANCE AND DRAMA

There are a number of dance schools throughout the country, the most famous of which is the Royal Ballet School at White Lodge in Windsor Great Park.

The overriding importance of careful, corroborated, expert assessment before a youngster is committed to a specialist ballet course at the age of 8 parallels that of the selection of young violinists. Indeed, there are additional physical factors which apply in the case of classical ballet. For, given all the talent in the world, if a young girl's make-up is such that she is bound to be tall and overweight by the time she is 18, it is better not to begin or to try contemporary dance instead. Such outcomes can be prognosticated medically and so careful physiological assessment is also vital in initial selection.

As far as the academic and boarding aspects of ballet school life are concerned, they must match the criteria for all schools for the same age group. As with the specialist music schools there are additional necessary criteria. These include the following:

1. good teachers of classical ballet or the dance form being studied;
2. occasional supervision by a noted exponent;
3. opportunities for regular practice;
4. ready access to a physiotherapist (in case of injury);

5. opportunities to see dance performances of the highest quality;
6. opportunities to perform for a variety of audiences in a variety of roles and different sized groups;
7. exemption from other forms of school exercise or games, particularly those that may place the limbs at risk.

There are few purely drama schools for secondary age pupils, but one should mention the Arts Educational Schools at Tring and Chiswick which offer a curriculum including academic subjects together with substantial timetabled provision of art, music, dance and drama, and the opportunity to specialise later in one of these fields. As might be expected, both schools have relevant specialist staff and facilities which have to meet all the criteria of other dance and music schools, and they have in addition studios for art and theatre facilities for drama. Interestingly, the value of this broad aesthetic programme appears greater than the simple sum of these performance areas. Capable students have the choice of carrying more than one specialism, but also extensive interaction between these areas is mutually enriching and introduces students to cross-disciplinary works of musical theatre, opera, dance drama, as well as the purely dance, drama or musical works.

We have spent this chapter looking at a few rather different trees in the educational wood and at the distinctive attention these sometimes need. But we must not lose sight of the wood for the trees for in the end schools and trees both have far more similarities than differences.

Just as all trees need light, air, food, space, congenial climate and good forestry, so in assessing schools we look above all for a good match between what the school can provide and what each child needs; for high qualities of intellectual nurture, personal care and individual encouragement as these apply to all the pupils; for principled leadership and vision which comprehends and is comprehended by staff and pupils alike; and above all for space to flourish.

Bibliography

DES publications (obtainable from HMSO)

Better Schools, A Summary (1985).
National Curriculum 5–16, A consultative document (1987).
National Curriculum Task Group on Assessment and Testing – A Report (1987).
A digest of the preceding (1987).
New Perspectives on the Mathematics Curriculum (Cambridge Institute of Education) (1985)
Mathematics Counts: Report of the Committee of Enquiry into the Teaching of Mathematics in Schools (Dr WH Cockcroft) (1982).
Report of the Committee of Enquiry into the Teaching of English Language (Sir J Kingman) (1988).
Ten Good Schools – A Secondary School Enquiry (1977).

APU publications

Free publications available from APU Unit, DES, Elizabeth House, York Road, London SE1 7PH.

SURVEY REPORTS
Mathematics
'Primary Surveys 1, 2, 3' (1978, 1979, 1980) NFER-Nelson.
'Secondary Surveys 1, 2, 3' (1978, 1979, 1980) NFER-Nelson.
'Review of Monitoring in Mathematics' (1978–1982) HMSO.
'Foreign Language' (1985) NFER-Nelson.

Language performance in schools
'Primary Survey' (1979, 1980) NFER-Nelson.
'Secondary Surveys' (1982) NFER-Nelson.

'Language Performance in Schools' (1979) HMSO.

Science in schools
The following are published by ASE, College Lane, Hatfield, Herts:
'Report 1, Ages 11, 13, 15' (1980).
'Report 2, Ages 11, 13, 15' (1981).
'Report 3, Ages 11, 13, 15' (1982).
'Report 4, Ages 11, 13, 15' (1983).

Summary reports on all the above are available free from the APU, DES. Parallel Welsh reports corresponding to the above are also available from the same sources.

'Assessment in USA' (1979) free from the APU. National and State Assessment in the USA (Prof P Black/DTE Marjoram)

OCCASIONAL PAPERS
'No 3 Standards of Performance' (1984) free, APU.

SHORT REPORTS
On science Nos 1–9 are available, priced, from ASE.

On language on Speaking and Listening
                   Assessment of Writing
                   Assessment of Reading
are available, priced, from NFER-Nelson.

On mathematics on Decimals
                      Practical mathematics
                      The Cockcroft Foundation⎫ NFER-Nelson.
                      List   ⎭

On foreign languages on Assessing⎫
                            Writing ⎬ NFER-Nelson.
                            Speaking ⎭

NEWSLETTERS
Nos 1–9 from spring and autumn 1982–1987 are available from APU.

LEAFLETS
'Assessing the Performance of Pupils' (Reports on Education Series) (1978) APU.
'Monitoring Maths, Science Languages, Foreign Languages', APU.

85

Mathematics:
    Length
    Area and Perimeter } Priced sets, HMSO
    Lines and Angles

SAMPLE QUESTION BOOKLETS
On language, science, mathematics, available free, from APU.

POPULAR
How well can 15 year olds write?', free, APU.

The most recent APU publications for 1988 include:
Reviews of APU Survey Findings 1980–84 for:

    Science at Age 11, ASE.
    Science at Age 13, ASE.
    Science at Age 15, ASE.

together with a Technical Review and an Independent Appraisal of
APU. Findings in Science 1980–84.

Short reports on
Science   'Science Report for Teachers No. 10 : Metals at Age 15',
        ASE.

Language   'Pupils' attitudes to writing', NFER-Nelson.
        'Pupils' attitudes to reading', NFER-Nelson.

Mathematics   'Attitudes and Gender Differences', NFER-Nelson.

Foreign languages   'Listening and Reading', NFER-Nelson.

Leaflets
Language   'Writing by Design', APU.
        'Reading for Reference', APU.
        'Who Enjoys Writing?,' APU.

HMI publications

HM Inspectors of Schools:
   'Their purpose and role' (1988).

Reporting Inspections:
   'HMI Methods and Procedures' (1986).
   'Maintained Schools' (1986).

Reporting Inspections:
'HMI Methods and Procedures' (1986).
'Independent Schools' (1986).

Education Observed:
'A review of the first six months of published reports by HM Inspectors' (1984).

Education Observed 2:
'A review of HMI reports on primary schools and 11–16 and 12–16 comprehensive schools' (1984).

Education Observed 3:
'Good teachers' (1985).

Education Observed 4:
'Homework' (1987).

Education Observed 5:
'Good behaviour and discipline in schools' (1987).

'10th Report by HMI on LEA provision for education and the quality of response in schools and colleges in England' (1986)

All the above publications are free and are available from the DES Publications Despatch Centre, Honeypot Lane, Stanmore, Middlesex HA7 1AZ.

The priced publications which follow can, like all DES publications, be ordered from HMSO Books (P9D), Freepost, Norwich NR3 1BR.

The Curriculum from 5 to 16, Curriculum Matters 2 (1985).
English from 5–16, Curriculum Matters 1 (1986).
Mathematics from 5–16, Curriculum Matters 3 (1987).
Music from 5–16, Curriculum Matters 4 (1985).
Home Economics 5–16, Curriculum Matters 5 (1985).
Health Education 5–16, Curriculum Matters 6 (1986).
Geography 5–16, Curriculum Matters 7 (1986).
Modern Foreign Languages to 16, Curriculum Matters 8 (1987).
Craft, Design and Technology 5–16, Curriculum Matters 9 (1987).
Careers Education and Guidance 5–16, Curriculum Matters 10 (1988).
Quality in Schools: Evaluation and Appraisal (1985).
Quality in Schools: The Initial Training of Teachers (1987)
Education in the Federal Republic of Germany (1986).
Aspects of Primary Education in the Netherlands (1987).
Art in Secondary Education 11–16 (1983).

History in the Primary and Secondary Years (1985).
Records of Achievement at 16 (1985).
Primary Schools – Some Aspects of Good Practice (1987).
Education 8–12 in Combined and Middle Schools HMI Survey (1985).
9–13 Middle Schools – An illustrative Survey (1983).
Education 5–9: An Illustrative Survey of 80 First Schools in England (1982).
Aspects of Secondary Education: A Survey by HM Inspectors of Schools HMI Survey (1979).
Primary Education in England: HMI Survey (1978).
Experiencing A Level – Aspects of Quality (1987).
Secondary Schools, An Appraisal by HMI (1988).

LEA publications

Devon Working Party Report *The Arts in Schools* (1987)
ILEA Learning Materials Service *Keeping the School under Review:*
The Primary School (1983).
The Secondary School (1983).
The Special School (1983).
ILEA *Improving Secondary Schools* (1984).
ILEA *Improving Primary Schools* (1985).

Other publications

Association of Teachers of Mathematics (ATM) (1988) *National Curriculum in Mathematics – A Summary and Commentary* (by Noel Fowler).
Barry, H and Tye, F (1972) *Running a School*, Temple Smith.
Blishen, E (ed) (1969) *The School That I'd Like,* Penguin Educational Special.
Blood, DF and Budd, WC (1972) *Educational Measurement and Evaluation*, Harper & Row.
Broadfoot,P, James,M, McMeeking, S, Nuttall, D and Stierer, B (1988) *Records of Achievement. Report of the National Evaluation of Pilot Schemes*, HMSO.
Burns,JM (1978) *Leadership*, Harper and Row, NY.
Chartered Institute for Public Finance and Accountancy (1988) *Performance Indicators for Schools*.
Clift, P, Macintosh, H and Nuttall, D (1981) *Measuring Learning Outcomes*, Open University Press.

Close, G and Brown, M (1988) *Graduated Assessment in Mathematics*, Secondary Schools Curriculum Council (SSCC).

(A brief summary of the above is also available from the DES Publications Despatch Unit.)

DES (1983) *The Work of HM Inspectorate in England and Wales.*

DES (1983) *HM Inspectors Today: Standards in Education.*

Gipps, C (1983) *Testing Children*, Heinemann Educational Books.

Greenbaum, W (1977) *Measuring Educational Progress*, McGraw-Hill.

Harlen, Wynne (1978) *Evaluation and the Teacher's Role*, Macmillan.

Harris, D and Bell, C (1986) *Evaluating and Assessing for Learning*, Kogan Page.

Holt, J (1970) *The Underachieving School*, Pelican.

Hopkinson, D (1981) *Edward Penrose Arnold, A Victorian Family Portrait*, Alison Hodge.

Howe, A and Spiro, B (1987) *School Report*, Weidenfeld and Nicholson.

Incorporated Association of Preparatory Schools (IAPS) (1987) *Notes for the Guidance of Governors and Members.*

Kynnersley, EM Sneyd (1930) *HMI's Notebook*; or *Recreations of an Inspector of Schools*, John Lane, London.

Lewis, DG (1974) *Assessment in Education*, ULP.

Lewis, R (1984) *How to Help Learners Assess Their Progress*, CET.

Mathematical Association (MA) (1979) *Evaluation: of What, By Whom, For What Purpose?*

Mortimore, P, et al (1988) *School matters – the Junior Years*, Open Books Publishing Ltd., Wells, Somerset.

Nuttall, DL (1981) *School Self Evaluation – Accountability with a Human Face?*, Schools Council.

Open University (1988) *Review of 56 Schools Operating Their Own Review or Appraisal Schemes.*

Pidgeon, DA (1972) *Evaluation of Achievement*, Macmillan.

Poster, CD (1976) *School Decision Making*, Heinemann Educational Books.

Shipman, M (1979) *In-School Evaluation*, Heinemann Educational Books.

Swinburne, AJ (1912) *Memoirs of a School Inspector. Thirty-five Years in Lancashire and Suffolk*, Published by author at Saxmundham.

Thompson, F (1939) *Lark Rise*, OUP.

Index